BLACK BIBLE CHRONICLES SERIES
THE GOSPELS

Rappin' with Jesus
The Good News According to The Four Brothers

P. K. McCary
Interpreter

African American Family Press

AFRICAN AMERICAN FAMILY PRESS™
An imprint of Multi Media Communicators, Inc.
575 Madison Avenue, Suite 1006
New York, NY 10022

Cover design by Jason Gamke

Cover illustration by Tim Ladwig

Black Bible Logo by Tim Ladwig

Library of Congress Cataloging-in-Publication Data

McCary, P. K., 1953-

Rappin' with Jesus: the good news according to the four brothers / P. K. McCary, interpreter.—1st ed.
    p.   cm.—(Black Bible Chronicles: 2)
ISBN 1-56977-005-0 (pbk.): $14.95
1. Bible. N.T. Gospels—Paraphrases. 2. Black English—Juvenile literature. [1. Bible stories—N.T.] I. Title. II. Series: McCary, P. K. 1953- Black Bible Chronicles; 2.
BS2557.M34 1994
226'.05209—dc20   93-71549
                                                  CIP
                                                  AC

First Edition

10 9 8 7 6 5 4 3 2

Printed in the United States of America

For My Children
Malik, Eryon and Jarian

There was pow'r—pow'r,
wonder working pow'r
in the precious Blood of the Lamb!

Spiritual

FOREWORD
Rappin' with Jesus

It is my honor to be asked to write the foreword to the second book in the *Black Bible Chronicles* series, *Rappin' With Jesus: The Good News According to the Four Brothers.*

In the foreword I wrote for the first book in the series, *Black Bible Chronicles: From Genesis to the Promised Land,* I stated my support for this project, which brings the Word of God to our younger generation in contemporary language.

Modern people often think of the story of Jesus and his mission as a remote piece of history with little relevance to today's problems. Indeed the challenges of the 90s are of staggering proportions. In addition to a prolonged economic slowdown, our cities continue to cry out for attention, our youth are confused, lacking hope in far too many cases. Violence is commonplace, and on and on.

Historically the gospel or *Good News* has been a powerful message of hope in the midst of despair, of light in the midst of utter darkness. Jesus reminds us that a few dedicated to His service can change lives and transform society.

P. K. McCary in her second offering in the *Black Bible Chronicles* series offers us yet another powerful interpretation of the Scriptures. *Rappin' with Jesus* is stunning and relevant, particularly to our young people who are hungry for spiritual food, yet need to understand it in terms meaningful to them in their unique culture and language.

Some in my generation will find *Rappin' with Jesus* off-putting and at times perplexing, but to our youth it can offer a doorway to understanding the significance of life in relationship with a personal God.

I applaud this book and hope that every young person will have the opportunity to glean from its riches, for indeed Christ came to bring life and life abundant.

The Honorable Andrew Young
Former Ambassador to the United Nations
Former Congressman and Mayor of Atlanta

CONTENTS

The Word According to Matthew

Matthew was a tax collector who decided to follow Jesus when He started preaching. He was called a disciple of Jesus and wrote these chapters 'cuz he felt that Jesus fulfilled the stories told more than four hundred years before.

Jesus Is Coming To Town

After more than fourteen generations, the time had come and a brother named Jesus arrived on the scene. Many righteous folks had told of His coming to save the world, but few knew what it was all about. He was gonna be a brother whose legacy went all the way back to his kinfolk, David the King. Even further, it went all the way back to Abraham, the Almighty's right-on brother.

It all went down like this.

A sister named Mary was to be married to a brother whose name was Joseph. It was Joseph, you see, who was a descendant of Abraham. It turned out that Mary was already pregnant, and Joseph, wasn't happy about it— especially since the kid wasn't his.

But, Joseph was a pretty cool brother. Although he coulda dissed the sister big time and had her sent away, he decided that Mary was an all right sister (although she *did* have a big problem). For her sake, he decided that he wasn't gonna tell everybody her business.

So while he sat and thought about just how he would send Mary away without everybody knowing what was happenin', an angel of the Almighty stood before him.

"Brother man, don't do this thing you're thinking. Believe me when I tell you, the kid Mary is carrying is a holy kid. Just like a brother named Isaiah said a long time ago, 'A virgin will get pregnant, though not by any brother, and when the kid is born His name shall be called *Immanuel*,' which is the name of the Almighty Hisself!"[1]

---

[1] See Isaiah, Chapter 7, verse 14.

And Joseph went, "That's pretty hip." Without another word, he married the sister, Mary, and when the kid was born they called the little brother, Jesus.

Brothers From The East

Jesus was born in a little town called Bethlehem 'round the time this dude named Herod was king. Three wise brothers heard 'bout the little brother's birth, too, 'cuz it had been said a really righteous King of the Jews would be born. And King Herod was a bit upset about what he was hearing, especially when he considered himself the only king!

"Who is this brother ya'll talking 'bout?" he asked his boys, the big time priests and historians.

And they told him, "Right in Bethlehem of Judea, the talk is that something big is going down. It says right here," the historians pointed out. "'Right in the heart of Bethlehem a What's Happenin' Brother will come to lead the Almighty's people.'"

Ol' Herod was slick. After he heard about this little brother, he called the wise men to him on the sly and told 'em, "Listen, go and look for the kid everybody's talkin' 'bout and let me know where he is. I, uh, wanna lay something on Him."

But the wise brothers were hipped to what was really on Herod's mind. They set out to look for the child, taking with them gifts and fine things. Following a big, bright star, they found the child and gave him gold, frankincense and myrrh.[2] When they left, they each had a dream that

---

[2]These were types of fragrances that made really cool incense.

told them they best be not telling ol' Herod anything. So, without a word, they took the back road home, bypassing Herod's place altogether.

But on the side of town where Joseph and his family slept, the angel of the Almighty came to Joseph in a dream.

"Hey, man. Get up. Now! You gotta get your wife and the little brother outta here. That bad ol' King Herod wants to waste the kid, so take everybody to Egypt until things cool down."

And no one had to tell Joseph twice. He was outta there in a flash. He and his family lay low in Egypt until ol' Herod was dead in his grave. And when they headed out of Egypt, it was just like a prophet named Hosea had told folk hundreds of years before. "Outta Egypt the Almighty called His son."[3] That son was none other than the little brother Jesus, the babe born in Bethlehem.

Herod really wanted to waste this little brother, and before he kicked the bucket, he wreaked some serious havoc on the little town of Bethlehem and all 'round and about those parts. He was really mad that the three brothers with the gifts had been truly wise.

"Who are they to diss me this way?" Herod roared. "I tell you what. If they ain't gonna be down with my program, we'll leave no stone unturned." And with that said, Herod ordered that every little brother under the age of two was to be wasted. And it was a drive-by night in Bethlehem as Herod wasted a lot of little brothers. It was just like a brother named Jeremiah had said long time

---

[3]See Hosea, Chapter 11, verse 1.

ago, "It was a hard time in Ramah, lots of crying and moaning.   Rachel cried for her kids 'cuz they was no more."[4]

And even after Herod was rotting in his grave, Joseph and his family didn't return to Bethlehem. He heard that a brother named Archelaus was running things and that brother scared him just as much as Herod had. So the Almighty told Joseph to go and be down in a little place called Galilee.   And settling in the town of Nazareth, Joseph and Mary raised little Jesus.

A Wild Brother Named John

There was this really wild brother people called John the Baptist, and he ran 'round in the wilderness of Judea telling brothers and sisters to "Get your act together 'cuz the Almighty's program is just about to happen."

And just like a brother named Isaiah told the folks more than four hundred years before, "The voice of a brother will be heard out in the wilderness saying, 'Get ready 'cuz He's comin'."[5]

John was a really weird dude. He ran 'round dressing real soulful in camel's hair clothing, with a leather belt 'round his waist. And to top it off, the brother ate locusts (kinda like grasshoppers) and honey.

John the Baptist didn't take no mess. He baptized those who came out to him by dunking them in water, but he

---

[4]See Jeremiah, Chapter 31, verse 15. Ramah is another name for Bethlehem.
[5]See Isaiah, Chapter 40, verse 3.

warned those swoll-headed Pharisees[6] and Sadducees[7] to look out.

"Who told you that the Almighty was comin' down hard, you wanna-be brothers? Who tol' you?" John asked.

And those brothers slid their feet back and forth, staring at the ground.

"That's what I thought," he admonished them. "You go 'round tellin' folk, 'I'm a big shot. I'm one of the Almighty's chosen,' but it don't mean nothing. The Almighty can get anybody to get down with His program. He don't need you. I tell you what. He's got the ax and if the tree ain't bearing any fruit, down it comes." And John The Baptist laughed at 'em.

"But if you're really sorry, I'll baptize you with water. It's the best I can do, but there's a brother comin' whose sandals I ain't fit to wear and when He comes on the scene, He'll baptize you with the Holy Spirit of the Almighty. It'll be like fire and lightnin'—I tell you, the way He'll be down will be frightenin'. That is, if you ain't with it." So, John went on to explain that this brother would come and clean the place up like never before.

Later, right there at the Jordan river where John stood, came the brother named Jesus who asked John to baptize Him.

"Oh, man. You gotta be kidding. Me? Baptize *you?* Man, you got that wrong. You got the power."

---

[6]The Pharisees were the religious honchos. Some were very religious teachers.
[7]The Sadducees were the aristocrats or the really rich. They believed only in the law of Moses.

And Jesus answered him, *"Don't sweat it, man. For now, this is the way it's gotta be to fulfill the word that's gone before us."*

And when John had baptized Him, immediately the heavens burst open and the Almighty's spirit came down on Him like a dove, resting all 'round His shoulders. A smooth, thunderous voice filled the skies and said, *"This is my beloved son, and He pleases Me greatly."*

The Devil Went Down To Galilee

The Spirit led Jesus up from the little Jordan river and further up in the wilderness to go one-on-one with Satan. And for forty days and nights, Jesus didn't eat anything, so he was hungry.[8]

And that bad ol' devil came to tempt Jesus into doing something wrong.

"Hey, brother man. If you are *really* the Almighty's kid, say the word and tell these stones to become bread."

And Jesus answered him. *"It is written that a brother can't live by bread alone. It takes every word the Almighty lays down."*

And the devil was clever. He grabbed Jesus and took him up to the top of a building and made him look down.

"Come on. Make like Superman and fly. 'Cuz it says in that word you talkin' about that the Almighty got angels who will take care of you and are strong enough to carry you so that you won't get crushed on the stones. It says that, don't it?"

---

[8]To go without eating for a long period is called a fast.

And again Jesus told that ol' devil, *"I'll tell you what is written. It says 'don't tempt the Almighty, your Master.'"*

That ol' devil snarled and snorted, but he didn't give up. "Okay, you're so cool. Have a look at this." And he took Him high up on a mountain and showed Him the wonders of the world. Big, golden cities lay before Him.

"You can have all this, my brother, if you just fall down and worship me," he said slyly. "Think about it."

And once and for all, Jesus gave that devil what for. *"Get behind me, Satan. You ain't nothing. Scripture says that a brother should only serve the Almighty and Him alone. Now git!"*

And the devil had no choice. When you gotta go, you gotta go. As soon as he had left, the Almighty sent angels to take care of the brother, Jesus, who was really tired and worn out.

Jesus chilled after wrestling with the devil, so it wasn't until He got back that He heard His friend, John, had been taken to jail, so He went to Galilee to see what was up. From Nazareth He left to go and sit awhile in Capernaum, by the sea between Zebulun and Naphtali. It was just like the prophet Isaiah had said, "And between Zebulun and Naphtali, just 'round the bend from the river Jordan, the folks who sat out in the dark looked over and saw a bright light. Even those in the valley of death, saw dawn on the horizon."[9] And from that moment in time, the brother Jesus was called to preach saying, *"Tell the Almighty you're sorry, 'cuz His time is right now."*

---

[9]See Isaiah, Chapter 9, verses 1 and 2.

As Jesus walked out by the Sea of Galilee, He ran into two brothers, Simon (they called him Peter), and Andrew, fishing out on the pier. He walked over to them and said, *"Follow Me and you'll be fishers of brothers."*

And why, it don't matter, but the brothers lay down their nets and followed Him. From there they saw two others, James and his brother, John, in the boat with their daddy. Jesus called to them, too. Without any hesitation they joined Jesus and the others to teach and preach to the brothers and sisters 'bout the Almighty's program.

But the greatest thing of all, was Jesus could heal the sick. If you were sweating any type of sickness, dealing with devils 'round you, or couldn't walk, talk, or see, Jesus could say the word and it was right side up again.

And brothers and sisters started following Him, just to get a peek at Him, just to touch Him once. From Galilee to Decapolis, 'round to Jerusalem and Judea—all along the coast of Jordan, Jesus' rep was solid.

Jesus Raps With the Brothers On the Hill

One day as folks were starting to press all 'round Jesus, He decided to go up on a hill for a minute to rap with His chosen brothers.[10] He wanted them to know what was up.

"You know, there's a little something for everybody," Jesus told 'em. *"Brothers who are down in the way the feel, they ain't got nothing to worry 'bout 'cuz the Kingdom of Heaven belongs to them. Even those who feel like*

---

[10]The brothers who followed Jesus were called disciples and Jesus taught them like students in school.

they've lost, can be on the one again 'cuz there will be arms 'round 'em to make 'em feel better. And you know those brothers who seem weak and on the bottom of the tadpole, the world is theirs. No kidding. And those folks who always do right, got a kind word to say, a good deed or two to do, it's coming back to 'em in spades. If a brother shows kindness and mercy, it's coming back to him more than he can count. Righteousness is given to those whose hearts are pure and good, for in the end they shall see the Almighty. And those that keep the peace, my brothers, shall be called the Almighty's children. But, those who are dissed and stepped on 'cuz they are trying to do the right thing, the kingdom of heaven is theirs. And here's the kicker," Jesus told them. "If you have to suffer 'cuz you're my main brothers, no matter what it is, you gotta know that in the end, the ultimate is gonna be laid on you. It'll be worth more than gold.[11]

"Look, this is for real. My brothers, you're gonna be the salt of the earth. And you know that salt ain't no good to nobody if there's no flavor left. Might as well throw it out, but this ain't gonna happen.

"You will be the light of the world. Won't be no hiding places. If you put a city on a hill, everybody gets a peek, right? You don't put a light under a basket, do you? No, you put a shade on top and it lights up the house. This is what I'm trying to tell you guys. You gotta let your light shine so that brothers can see what's happenin' with each of you. You gotta let your light shine."

---

[11]Read and study the Beatitudes in Matthew, Chapter 5, verses 3 through 12.

And then Jesus laid it out like this for them. He wanted them to know how He came to be here and why He chose them in the first place.

"I ain't come here to try and change the Law or what the brothers have been saying for hundreds of years. No sir! I'm here to make what they say on the one!

"We can't go forward 'til everything that has been foretold has been done. Look, Moses had things down pat, I grant you. And anyone who tries and breaks the law gonna get what's comin' to 'im. It's that simple. If you can't do the time, don't do the crime. Got it? But here's the real deal.

"I know you believe in the Almighty. But if you can't be better than those Pharisee brothers and those other so-called head honchos, you won't have to sweat going to heaven. It ain't happenin'.

"Murder is still murder, baby, but there's more. You try sweating a brother for no reason, you're still guilty. And you know how easy it is to rank on a brother, calling him stupid or worse, a fool. It's gotta stop. I'm not changing laws, my brothers, I'm adding to 'em. Hell itself will be on your doorstep otherwise.

"When you go to church to pray and give thanks and an offering, stop a minute and think. Need to fix somethin' with your brother or sister? Somebody you been sweatin' or been sweating you? Better do it first before coming to the Almighty 'cuz that gift don't mean nothing to Him otherwise.

"And those who diss another brother saying, 'He ain't nothing' just 'cuz you consider him an enemy need to get straight yourself. I'm tellin' you, don't go to hell just 'cuz you've disagreed with some brother and you ain't speaking. Fix it, no matter who's at fault.

"You brothers who go 'round peeping and pointing at the sisters, thinking, 'I ain't doing nothing wrong 'cuz I ain't down with her,' think again. Whether for real or in your mind, it's all the same to the Almighty 'cuz it was done in your heart.

"Look, if that ol' bad eye keeps turning the wrong way, it's better to take it out than to go to hell for peeping. Your hand starts touching, your feet start walking. If it's wrong, it's better to go to heaven with part of you missing than all of you in hell.

"Divorce has been too easy these days. Look out. No more handing out divorce papers like yesterday's news. If she ain't been running 'round on you, both of you are headed on a one-way ticket to you know where. It's all the same, even if you marry someone who has been divorced this way, it ain't cool at all.

"It's also been said that you don't want to go 'round swearing that you're gonna do this and that when you don't mean it, but I'm tellin' you, don't swear at all. Don't go 'round saying, 'I swear on the Almighty that I'll do it,' 'cuz even if you do it, you've used the Almighty's name in a way that ain't right. No way. Not even on somebody's else's name or head. Who are you? You can't make nobody's hair white or black. If someone backs you in a corner, just say 'yes' if you mean to do it, and 'no' if you don't."

But Jesus wasn't through. He didn't miss a beat as He laid out His plan for the brothers up there on the hill.

"Some folks say, 'an eye for an eye, a tooth for a tooth,' and you know what that means? I hear 'em. 'Man, if he *puts a hurting on me, I'm gonna jack him up.' I'm telling you no in no uncertain terms. If he slaps the dog stuffing outta you, turn the other cheek. If he takes your jacket, give him your scarf too. He takes you outta your way a mile or two, add another. Don't turn the brother away if he needs you. Be there for him.*

"And it's also been said that you should love your brother man, but hate the brother that disses you big time, but here's the real deal. Love your enemies, man. Don't turn 'em out. Those that spit on you and use you to the last drop, have a heart with 'em. There's a good reason for it all.

"When you can love the one who does you the most harm, you brothers will be sons of the Almighty. Ain't that kickin'? It's easy to love someone who loves you. So what? What does it mean? Not a thing. But if you can love someone who is hard to love, someone who just seems the worst brother around, I'm tellin' you that you will be on the one. Perfecto in these hard times."

This Little Light of Mine...

Jesus wanted the brothers to know just what they were getting into. He didn't want no misunderstandings as this thing got underway.

"Look, I want you to do good things, but I don't want you showboating. Ain't nothing happenin' to brothers who do good things for show. It's like this, you know those brothers who call a press conference every time they do somethin' good. Somehow, it gets in the news. It ain't what's happenin'.

"It won't have the same impact when everybody knows what you're doing. Keep a lid on it and I promise you, the Almighty has got eyes in the back of His head. What you do in secret is on the Heavenly news and that's what counts.

"And even when you pray, don't go on stage. Have a little dignity. You know how some folks pray in the church: 'Lord, that Sister Smith or Brother Jones sho can pray.' Well, that might be true, but remember that the Almighty sees right smack into your heart. If you ain't for real, he'll know it. Better to be yourself and pray something like this:

> "Our Father in heaven, Your name is so wonderful. We want Your kingdom right now, but it's gotta be what You want, both here on earth and in heaven. Right now we're asking that You give us that day to day thing that You do so well, nourishing and feeding us, but forgive us for being so sinful. And just like You forgive us, we'll forgive each other 'cuz that's what You said. And one more thing, Lord, we ask that You put a hold on those things that tempt us to diss You and do wrong 'cuz the devil is on the loose. Deliver us from him. Amen!

And the Almighty will forgive you just that quick, but not if you don't forgive your brothers and sisters out there.

"And when you fast for a while don't go 'round looking all sad and pitiful so everyone knows what's up. No, clean yourself up. Put a smile on your face. I'm tellin' you, those that put on those kinds of acts will get what's comin' to 'em. Only the Almighty needs to know what's going on.

"And you material girls and boys, trying to live this life lavishly, I'm here to tell you that you better be trying to gain stock in heaven where it really adds up. What's all this gold on earth that over time just becomes junk? Nothing, I tell you.

"If you let the light of the Almighty shine through, everything you are will be clear as a bell. If there's darkness in your eye, your life will be dark as well.

"So make up your mind. You can't have it both ways. Either you're gonna follow the Almighty and Me, or you ain't. You can't go 'round dressed to the nines. We've got work to do.

"So, here's the deal in black and white. Don't worry 'bout nothing, not what you'll eat or drink or even where you'll be staying. This life, your life, is worth more than food and clothes and fine hotels and the like. Look up and see the birds. The Almighty has always taken care of them. He'll take care of you. You won't have to worry 'bout nothing if you follow Me.

"Look at the lilies out there in the field. They grow strong and pretty and they don't worry about where the light or rain is comin' from, do they? You think Solomon[12] was dressed finer than that? I don't think so. The Almighty has been dressing the earth longer than you can remember, further than time itself. Ain't nobody ever done it better.

"So, it's like this, my brothers. Don't ask the questions, 'What shall we wear? What shall we eat? Where shall we stay?' Look toward the Almighty and His

---

[12]Solomon was one tough Hebrew King. His dad was King David and Solomon was usually decked out in fine jewelry and threads.

program, and these other things you worry 'bout will be there. Don't go 'round worrying 'bout tomorrow, 'cuz it'll take care of itself and the Almighty will take care of you."

People In Glass Houses...

"You brothers kill me, you really do. Don't go 'round talking 'bout what a brother is or isn't doing when you might not be so hot yourself. How you gonna tell another brother how he should be doing something when you ain't doing nothing yourself. Those so-called specks in his eyes are like tree limbs in yours. You can't see nothing yourself.

"And you brothers always spouting off in front of anybody who will listen, I'm telling you not to give a good bone to a mangy dog. Don't take good advice and make it slop for the pigs. Get my drift? That ol' dog will only bury it and pigs will just trample it in the dirt anyway. What good is it?

"It's this simple. All you gotta do is ask. If you knock, the door will open. Anyone who really wants to know what's going down with the Almighty's program don't have to dibble and dabble, it's all right there, I promise you.

"Would you give your son a stone if he asked for some bread? I don't think so. If he wants to fry up some fish, you gonna hand him a snake? Look, you ain't nobody and you know how to give to those you love, so think how much more the Almighty can do than you? Be right by everyone and you'll be on the one with the Almighty.

"This road ain't easy to travel. You could easily travel down the road everybody is on, but what good would it do if the road goes to hell?

"You also gotta look out for those fast talking brothers who claim to be righteous. They're just wolves in sheep's clothing, man. All you gotta do is look 'round 'em. If they're on the one, you'll know it 'cuz good things will be happenin'. Good trees have juicy fruit. Say it ain't so? So look 'round 'em. If their people 'round them are righteous, they will be too!

"Believe this. Not everybody who goes 'round saying, 'Lordy, Lordy,' is going to heaven. If you ain't on His program, you ain't going nowhere. Those same folks will be saying in the end, 'Hey, Jesus, man. You know me. I preached in the churchhouse and held myself out to be a preacherman,' I'll tell the brother to git 'cuz I don't know him.

"So if you're listening to me, doing like I say, you will be like a brother who builds his house on a rock. Rain and thunder can't bring it down, but if you're silly and hardheaded and try building that house on sand, out into the ocean it will flow."

Now Jesus had told 'em just what His program was about and what He expected. He didn't want 'em having any doubts that He was the Man.

Miracle On "J" Street

So all was said and done, and Jesus and the brothers came down from the mountain straight into the crowd waiting for them. And this brother who was 'flicted with the lepers' disease came before Jesus begging Him to cure him.

"Brother Jesus, if you want to, please make me whole again."

And Jesus told him, *"Brother man, I ain't got a problem with that. You are healed."* And in a blink of an eye, the man was normal again, just at the words of Jesus.

Then Jesus told him, *"Look, man. Here's what I want you to do. Don't go 'round telling everybody 'bout this. Just go straight to the church and give an offering like Moses told folks to do long time ago. This is the law."*

Later when Jesus came into the town of Capernaum, an officer in the Roman army came to Jesus and begged, too, to have his employee healed.

"Lord, I got a real sick employee who is paralyzed and awful sick."

And before he could finish, Jesus said, *"I will come with you and cure him."*

But the officer stopped Him and said, "I ain't nobody to you, Jesus. I'm just a sorry brother who has a little action going for him. I can tell folks to come and go, but I don't want to trouble you. Just say the word and I know my employee will be cured."

And Jesus was really cool with the guy. He pointed out to the others what faith was all about.

"I'm tellin' you, I ain't heard this kinda faith ever, not even in Israel, but especially not 'round here. I'm tellin' you that folks gonna come from the east and the west and sit right long side Abraham, Isaac, and Jacob in heaven, but my brothers who the Almighty chose long ago, ain't going nowhere, but straight to hell!"

Jesus then turned to the Roman officer and told him, *"Go. It is just as you asked 'cuz you believed."* And when the officer got to his house, the employee was up and running just like Jesus had said.

That same day, Jesus went home for a bite with Peter and when they got there, Peter's mother-in-law was sick with fever. Quick as a flash, Jesus touched her hand and she rose, the fever broken, and fixed them something to eat.

In the evening, everybody was talking about Jesus. Folks were being brought to Him, left and right, to fix, to heal, to make feel better. And it was just like the prophets of old had said, "He would take our sicknesses on himself and bear them up."[13]

There were lots of people around Jesus so that He told the brothers that they needed to cross over to the other side of the lake. Before He could go, a Sunday school teacher came to Him and said, "Teacher, all you gotta do is ask and I will follow you."

Jesus told him, *"Foxes have holes and birds have nests, but I ain't got nowhere to lay my head."* And another brother said, "Lord, let me go and have a funeral for my dead father." Jesus told him, *"Let the dead bury the dead. Follow me."*

To cross over to the other side, Jesus got into a boat and along with Him the brothers who were following Him. Jesus fell asleep, but a great storm came and threw the boat around on the water. The brothers were plenty scared

---

[13]See Isaiah, Chapter 53, verse 4.

and didn't know how Jesus could sleep, so they woke Him up.

"You gotta save us. We're gonna die out here."

And Jesus just shook His head. *"Oh you silly brothers with no faith."* He then stood up and told the wind to hush and the sea to be still and the brothers were awestruck. "Who is this brother that can tell the wind and the waves to behave?"

When Jesus stepped out on the other side, He ran into two brothers who had the devil in them bad. These brothers were so strong that nobody messed with them or went near them at all. But when they saw Jesus, the demons on the inside of them were scared.

"Uh, oh," they cried. Over to the left was a herd of pigs, so the demons begged Jesus, "Look, at least send us in those pigs," 'cuz they knew their time was up in the bodies of the brothers. And Jesus said, *"Okay, so be it."* The demons went into the pigs and Jesus pointed His fingers at the pigs which started to run so fast, they ran right into the sea and drowned.

The brothers who had been keeping the pigs got scared and took off, too, and ran and told everybody what had happened. The townfolks were scared, so they asked Jesus to leave. "Please," they begged as nicely as they could.

So Jesus got back in the boat and went over to His hometown where He ran into a man who couldn't walk. The brother was lying out in the middle of the street on a bed. And Jesus said to him, *"Brother, don't be down. Your sins are forgiven you."*

And those so-called teachers standing 'round said that Jesus committed blasphemy![14]

"Who does this brother think he is?" they asked themselves. "He thinks he's the Almighty," others responded.

But if they thought they were talking where Jesus couldn't hear them, they were wrong. Jesus heard them all right and He had an answer for them.

"Oh, you think I don't know what you're saying and thinking? Tell me, which do you think is easier? To say, 'Your sins are forgiven,' or 'Get up and walk'? Huh? But since you wanna know who I am, here it is. I'm the Son of Man and I do have the power," He said as He turned to the brother down on the ground. Then He said, *"Get up, my man. Take your bed and go home."*

And the man took his bed and went home and when the townfolk saw what had gone down, they, too, were awestruck, and praised the Almighty for sending them Jesus.

Later, Jesus ran into a brother whose name was Matthew. For a living, Matthew collected taxes from the folks in town. Jesus told him, *"Follow me."*

Now after Matthew followed after Jesus, the two of them went over and sat with other tax collectors and the party folks in town, rapping and talking about what had gone down. Those wanna-be Pharisees, who saw themselves above everybody else, wanted to know what Jesus was doing if He was so high and mighty, talking with those *commoners!* But Jesus was good. He heard that, too, so He said to the Pharisee brothers, *"Those who don't need a*

---

[14]Blasphemy means to diss the Almighty.

doctor, ain't sick, and I'm 'bout sick of you. See if you can understand this. 'Have mercy and not sacrifice.'[15] *Look, I ain't come here to call on the righteous. If you're doing what's right, glad for you. I've come to call the party animals back to the Almighty."*

The brothers who had been following John the Baptist came to have a little talk with Jesus and they tole Him, "Your folks ain't going without no food. Nobody sees them fasting or nothing."

"You want them to go 'round sad when the bridegroom is with them? It'll be soon enough when I leave for them to fast. Would you put a new piece of unshrunk fabric on old clothes? Nah. The patch would tear away and make it worse. Would you put new wine into old jugs? I don't think so. It might leak and you'd lose the good wine. Put new on new and everything will be better, I promise."

While they were talking, one of the head honchos came and pleaded with Jesus to come with him and lay hands on his daughter who had just died.

"All you gotta do is put Your hands on her and she will live," he urged Jesus. "Please. Hurry."

And Jesus went with his disciples to do just that when suddenly a sister, who had been bleeding heavily for many years touched the hem of Jesus' garment. In her mind she believed that if she could only touch His garment, everything would be all right again.

---

[15]See Hosea, Chapter 6, verse 6, where the prophet Hosea warned folks that they should be about what the Almighty wants rather than all the pomp and circumstance.

Jesus turned and looked her straight in the eye. *"Don't be sad, my sister. Your faith has made you whole again."* The sister was made well from that very moment.

So, when Jesus came to the ruler's home, there were lots of folks around making noise, and kinfolk crying and carrying on. Jesus simply asked everybody to *"Get out 'cuz the girl ain't dead. She's just sleeping."* The folks laughed at him and made fun. But they were put out of the house. Once they were gone, Jesus put out His hand and the little sister rose from her bed like she had only been sleeping. And the news went out over the wire and everybody was talking 'bout Jesus.

After Jesus left there, He was followed by two blind men who cried, "Son of David, have mercy, man."

And Jesus asked them if they really believed He could heal them and they said, "Yeah, man. We do."

Then Jesus said, *"As you believe, that's the way it's gonna happen."* Then the blind men were made to see.

Later, a brother who couldn't say a word and had demons inside of him as well stood before Jesus. He cast the demons out and the man could talk. The townfolks were in awe. "Hey, He's the one all right. Ain't seen nothing like Him before." But the Pharisees weren't so sure. "He's casting out demons 'cuz He is one Himself," they told folks.

But Jesus wasn't worried about them. He went on with His program, healing the diseases and sicknesses of the folks just like He said He would. And the more He did, the more they came. Jesus felt real deep for them 'cuz the folks were like sheep with no shepherd to lead them. He looked out on His chosen brothers and told them, *"There's a lot of folks out there, but not enough workers to help.*

Bow down right now and help me pray to the Almighty to send us some more workers to help out 'round here. We could sure use it."

The Apostle Twelve

Now Jesus chose twelve brothers to run 'round with, preaching and teaching the Gospel. It was a gang of righteousness and each brother had the power, like no power before. Those brothers could tell that ol' devil to get lost, no matter what form he took; could heal the sick and those with diseases. Here are the names of the brothers: Simon (who the brothers called Peter), Andrew who was Peter's blood brother, James and John who were sons of Zebedee, Philip and Bartholomew, Thomas, Matthew, the tax collector, James whose dad was Alphaeus, and Labbaeus Thaddaeus, Simon from the town of Canaan, and Judas (who will put a hurtin' on Jesus later on). And Jesus took these brothers and molded and shaped them into a sin-fighting brigade.

"I am tellin' you I don't want you trying to run with the Gentiles or Samaritans, but look up your brothers and sisters of Israel. And tell folks that the Almighty's kingdom is real close, so close you can feel it.

"Heal the sick, clean up the lepers, raise the dead, tell that ol' devil and his demons that they're outta here, and whatever you've got to give, give it up freely.

"You don't have to carry gold and silver in your pockets 'cuz the Almighty's got your back. No need to pack a suitcase; leave the wardrobe at home in your closet. I'm tellin' you if you work hard, folks'll feed you.

"When you get to a new place, scout around and ask 'bout those folks that are in your corner. When they give

you a place to lay your head, bless their house when you enter. And if you find some fake brothers out there, just go your own way, taking your peace elsewhere.

"And more than that, some folks ain't gonna hear you, don't want to hear you, and that's OK. Just shake the dust offa you and keep steppin'. It'd be better that they lived in Sodom and Gomorrah than where they are for dissing you.

"But here's the real deal," Jesus told them. "It is gonna be rough. You'll be like sheep among wolves and, brother, that's rougher than rough. You gotta be as smart as a snake and as gentle as a dove.

"Watch out for brothers who talk outta both sides of their mouth 'cuz they'll stab you in the back every time. They'll set you up and you'll find yourself in front of some judge on trumped-up charges. And when that happens, just tell 'em 'bout Me and My Father, the Almighty. Even if they send you to jail, when you get to court, don't worry 'bout a lawyer or what your testimony will be. The Almighty, Hisself, will testify through you.

"It's only gonna get worse before it gets better. There'll come a time when a brother will stab another brother in the back, when fathers will stab their own children. Look—kids are gonna even waste their moms and dads. This is what's happenin' in the world today. And these same sinful folks will hate you, too. All because of Me! But if you stand, really stand, I won't let you down. The final analysis: you shall be saved.

"Look you might have to jump bail or get outta Dodge in a hurry 'cuz folks want to waste you. Just head to the next town. I'll be back before you can shake a stick.

"Understand the pecking order of things. A student can't rise above his teacher, and an employee can't rise

above his boss. But you really oughtta try and be as much like the teacher or boss as you can. Look, a lot of these folks call me Satan, himself, so you know what they'll think of you, but you can't let that worry you. It's like I've always said, whatever is done in the dark will certainly have to come to the light. These folks plotting to bring you down, gonna have the covers lifted off 'em. You wait and see. And anyway, you shouldn't be afraid of those brothers who can only kill the flesh 'cuz they can't touch your soul. Only the Almighty's got that power and don't you forget it.

"Ain't nothing gonna happen that the Almighty don't already know about. So don't sweat it. Okay? He knows about every sparrow in this world, and you're worth more than a bird. Every hair on your head is numbered and accounted for. He's got your back, always has, and always will.

"Call Me brother in front of others and I'll call you brother in front of My Father. Hey, but try dissing Me in public and I won't know your name in Heaven. Even though a brother will go against his father, a sister against her mother and a daughter-in-law against her mother-in-law, I'll make it work for good. Your enemies will be in your own home. If you love your mom and dad more than you love Me, then this ain't the gig for you. If you love your kids more than Me, don't even apply. You'll be fired before you're hired.

"If you want Me, you got Me. And when you got Me, you got the Almighty. Any brother or sister who takes a preacher in gonna reap big benefits. Not the money kind, but that which is worth more than gold. Even those who give a glass of water to one of my followers, his payback is wonderful indeed!

John The Baptist Places A Call

Jesus had just finished teaching His disciples and headed out to preach in different cities. John had gotten hipped in prison that Jesus was on the up-and-up and doing a bang-up job out there in the thick of it. So, he sent two of his group out to rap with Him 'cuz he had a few questions to put to the man.

"Are you the real deal, or should we keep looking?" John told his brothers to ask Jesus, so that they did. And Jesus answered, *"You just lay this on John. Tell him that the blind can see and the lame can walk. The deaf can hear and the dead rise and walk. I'm preaching the word to the poor, both in body and spirit. And everybody who takes heart, listens, and refuses to doubt Me will be blessed."*

Then Jesus turned to the crowd that had gathered and said, *"What did you think when you were jocking John out there in the desert? You think he was some raving maniac, or did you expect to see some sophisticated brother with gold dripping from his neck and fingers? You think he was a weak brother that the slightest wind would blow him over? Just what did you think? Well, I'll tell you who he was. He was the brother that prophets talked about for years before any of you were even born. He was My headliner, the opening act 'cuz this is what the Almighty told 'em:*

> *'Watch out 'cuz I'm gonna send an opening act before you who will set the stage for the main event.'[16]*

---

[16]See Malachi, Chapter 3, verse 1.

"And I'm here to tell you not one who has been born of a sister has been any heavier than John the Baptist. Here's the kicker though, 'cuz as great as John was, and don't get Me wrong, the Almighty said he was kicking, but those who ain't that heavy will be first among brothers. Understand that those who wrote about him, preached about him, need to know that John is Elijah, the one these brothers said would come when the Almighty's new program began. If you ain't listening, you better start.

"What can I say? You're like little kids running 'round talking 'bout one another. You say things like, 'We played at your wedding and you didn't dance, so we played at a funeral, but nobody was sad.' You called John crazy 'cuz he didn't eat and drink, and you call Me a party animal 'cuz I eat and drink and hang out with the brothers. You ain't even got your head on straight, and that weaving and bobbing don't mean nothing.

"Look, I've been a blessing to many. I've walked in cities and showed what the Almighty could do, but do folks turn to the Almighty? I'm telling you, in some cities, these brothers didn't even break a sweat when I worked the circuit. Other brothers tried to freeze Me out, and they ain't even sorry." And after all this was said and done, Jesus fell down on His knees and prayed.

"O Almighty God, head of Heaven and earth, I just wanna say thanks for not giving the lowdown to those folks that think they know everything. And thanks for opening the eyes of the ones who are young at heart, like little kids, who trust you and believe in you. You always did know what you were doing." And turning back to the crowd He said these words: *"I'm here 'cuz My Father sent me. Only the Almighty knows His son and the Almighty is*

known only by His son and those brothers I choose to reveal myself to. If you wanna come this way, I'll give you rest 'cuz I know the work ain't easy. Wear my bond and pledge 'cuz it is easy and I'll teach you the right way. With Me you'll find rest for your soul 'cuz My burdens are light."

Sunday A Day Of Rest

One Sunday Jesus and His men were in the fields. Since they were hungry, Jesus and the brothers pulled up some heads of grain to eat. And when the Pharisees (those wanna-be so righteous folks) saw what was happening, they started pointing fingers. "Hey," they yelled to Jesus. "What gives? Your men are out there working on a Sunday.[17] You know that ain't right."

Jesus looked them right in the eye and said, *"Don't you folks read? Remember what David and his buddies did when they were hungry? David went into the church and ate the special bread that only the preachers ate. And don't you know that preachers in Moses' day worked? You guys think you know so much, but if you did you'd know what the scriptures really say: 'You gotta have mercy, moreso than giving lots of money.' How dare you try and condemn My boys for getting something to eat when they were hungry. Don't you know I've got the power over every day of the week, including Sunday?"*

With that said, Jesus went into the church where a brother sat with a bum hand. And those Pharisees wanted to try and trick Jesus 'cuz they thought they were so smart.

---

[17]It was called the Sabbath Day, a Jewish day of worship. Although Jewish people celebrate the Sabbath on Saturday, most Christians view Sunday as the holy day.

"Tell us, Jesus. You think it's against the law to cure somebody on a Sunday?"

And Jesus answered them this way. *"You tell me, man? Which one of you would leave a sheep in a ditch on a Sunday? You wanna tell me you'd leave it in that ditch 'til Monday?"* And when they sat there looking stupid, He added, *"Isn't a brother worth more than a sheep? Yeah, it is lawful to do good on a Sunday. That answer enough for you?"* Then He turned to the man and told him to *"stretch out your hand."* And when the brother put out his hand, Jesus made it on the one again, just like his other one. But those swoll-headed Pharisees used what He had done to continue to gossip about Him in a negative way.

The thing is, Jesus knew it. He knew everything they said about Him. After He had cured the brother's hand, He took off, but the crowd still followed Him. He told them over and over again not to tell everybody His business, about where he was and where He was going. It was just like Isaiah the preacher had said hundreds of years before, "Look, this brother that I've chosen, has pleased Me greatly. I will put My Spirit on Him so that He can right wrongs, even to the Gentiles. He ain't gonna fuss and fight and many won't even hear Him when He speaks. Even if they whip His hide, He won't crack under the pressure 'til justice is done. And Gentiles will trust the name of Jesus in the end."[18]

And even after a brother had come to Jesus with demons that made him blind and unable to talk, the buzzword was that Jesus was the Son of David, come to

---

[18]See Isaiah, Chapter 42, verses 1 through 4.

save everybody. But those bad dudes didn't want folks to buy that. "Nah, He ain't the one. He's a demon himself fooling ya'll into believing that He's some kind of god. It ain't so."

Like it was said, Jesus knew what they were thinking. He even told them, *"You think I could destroy myself. A house divided ain't gonna stand no matter how you put it. You think a devil will put a devil out. Why? They're buddies, partners in crime. I do what I do by the Power of the Almighty, pure and simple. You can't even stand it, can you? It boils down to this. You're either with me or against Me.*

"Look I can forgive your dissing Me and doing wrong, 'cuz that's why I'm here, to try and save your butts. But when you diss the Almighty, especially in front of each other, it can't be forgiven. It's the ultimate in sinning.

"It's been said before, if the tree is good the fruit will be fine tasting. If the heart is good, good things will be said. Ain't nobody giving Me the benefit of the doubt even. They act like a bunch of snakes, always back-stabbing and cutting folks off at the knees. You want to call Me a devil, go ahead. But listen to Me good. Good brings good and evil brings evil. If you say I'm a devil and it ain't so, you'll have the devil to pay. But if you believe in Me, then your reward is the Almighty will believe in you."

Now the dudes weren't totally stupid. They asked for a sign and said, "Look, Mr. Man, the teacher, give us a sign. Show us."

And Jesus scoffed. *"You want a sign? Oh that's rich. You sinful, do-wrong brothers want a sign? I tell you what. You need a sign like the one Jonah got. Remember him? Three days and nights in the belly of a whale. Yep. Well, try My going down for three days and nights into the earth. Jonah came out after three days and so shall I. And I've got a power greater than My man, Jonah. And the brothers in Nineveh will be your judges. They finally had to listen to ol' Jonah. They could tell you a thing or two.*

"Even the Queen of Sheba knew better than you. The sister believed in idols and she came a thousand miles to hear Solomon and his wisdom. The wisdom of the Almighty. Yet, you diss Me. I tell you who has the demon. You! I come to cast out demons and they leave for a minute, but they come back every time and they find you without any substance so they bring their friends and each time it is worse than before 'cuz they bring seven of them bad dudes and they plan on staying a while. And that makes it worse than before. Look, who is My mom? Who is My dad? Who are My brothers? He then looked at His boys and pointed to them for all the folks, including the Pharisees to see. *"You see these brothers? They're my mother, father, and brother. They are everything to Me 'cuz they obey the Almighty who is My Father. You wanna know the real deal. I've said it. Can you dig it?"*

Talk That Talk

Now Jesus left and went down to the beach. Soon folks started following Him so that He had to go out into a boat so that there would be room. And from the boat He taught the folks about the Almighty, using little short stories[19] to get His point across. Like this one.

"There was this farmer who planted some seeds for grain on his farm. And as he sprinkled the seeds on the ground, some of the seeds went into ground that was kind of stony and rocky and not very deep. The seeds grew into plants all right, but because it wasn't buried very deep, the sun burned them to a crisp. Some of the seeds fell among the thorns and weeds so that when they started to grow, the thorns choked 'em to death. But some of the seeds fell on some really rich and fertile dirt and they grew by leaps and bounds, just like superseeds! You got ears, you got a mind, then you know what this story means."

But his boys didn't get it. "Hey, Jesus, sir, why do You tell us stories?"

Jesus looked at them and explained, *"You brothers can get what I'm sayin' here 'bout the Almighty's kingdom and all, but other brothers can't. I rap to them in stories 'bout stuff the brothers know. Since most of them are fishermen or farmers, I tell stories 'bout fishin' or 'bout the land.*

But some hardheaded brothers still won't pay attention or try to see where I'm comin' from. But you want to see," he told them. *"You want to know what the Almighty has in store for you. So here's the deal about the story. The part of the story where the seeds fell on hard ground is kind of like the person who hears the Word, but doesn't understand. The devil comes along and steals their very heart away. This man wants to know, but he ain't got no depth so it's a lost cause. The seeds that are planted in*

---

[19]The stories Jesus told were called parables. These were simple stories that made it easier for people to understand the Almighty's program.

thorny bushes is kind of like the man who goes to church every Sunday, hears the Word, but would rather live his life in the heaven he creates rather than the heaven of the Almighty. His wants and desires choke the love of the Almighty out of his very soul. But listen: The brother who hears the Word, understands it and goes out and tells others, whether thirty, sixty or a hundred, will get the real payback. The Almighty's got a payback to put a brother on easy street for eternity. I ain't talking about regular living, but the everlasting kind of living that only the Almighty can give."

And then He gave another example.

"A farmer planted his seeds good and deep in the soil. He took real good care of his crop. But one day this bad dude from another farm came and planted thorny weeds smack dab in the middle of his crop and before he knew anything, the soil was filled with good plants and thorns. The brothers that worked for the farmer wanted to know what they should do, but the farmer was cool 'cuz he knew that he used good fertilizer on his crop and had planted his seeds deep. He just told the brothers not to worry and to leave the thorns alone or they'd hurt the good plants. Don't worry, he told 'em. When the time came to harvest the plants, the farmer told his men to take the thorns and weeds and bundle 'em up for burning. And the good plants they harvested for the barn."

So, Jesus laid another story on them.

"The Almighty's kingdom is like the mustard seed. It's small, so small you almost can't see it. But it grows into a tree big enough for the birds." And still another story.

"The Almighty's kingdom is like a sister making bread. She kneads and pounds the bread until the yeast is all through it. And for all that pounding and kneading, when the bread comes out of the over, it's just right. Right like you will be."

Jesus explained that the preachers had said a long time ago, "He's gonna talk to them in stories that will end the mystery of what the Almighty's program." So, the rest of the day was spent telling stories. He compared Himself to a farmer.

"I'm the farmer. I've picked the best seeds and put them in the best ground. I've fertilized and watered them to grow, but somewhere the devil is busy and sends his demons to plant weeds, or brothers who ain't got nothing but evil on their minds. But when the harvest comes or the end of the world, with the help of angels, I'm gonna take my good strong plants and we're outta here. And those weeds, or brothers who think they're all this and that, will be burned, right along with the devil that planted 'em.

"The Almighty's kingdom is like a hidden treasure that a brother finds. The brother takes that treasure and hides it so he can go and sell everything he owns to buy the field where the treasure is hidden.

"The Almighty's kingdom is like a brother looking for pearls until he finds the perfect one. He'll sell everything he owns to have it.

"The Almighty's kingdom is like a fishnet that has been thrown into the sea. When you pull that net in it

brings in all sorts of things. So, you sit there, pulling the good to you, throwing the bad back.

"And that's the way it's gonna be in the end. The angels will come and pull the net in and the good they'll keep, but you know what happens to everything else not fit for the Almighty, don't you? Do you understand? 'Cuz this is really what's happenin'."

And later Jesus went to His hometown, but the brothers there remembered Him as Joseph and Mary's son. "Ain't that the carpenter's boy? Who does he think he is, spouting off wise words and trying to preach. I remember him when he wasn't nobody." So Jesus left, "'cuz a brother can get respect everyplace else, but home." And He didn't do much in His hometown 'cuz folks didn't believe.

Herod Wastes John The Baptist

Herod the king wasted John the Baptist 'cuz John told him it wasn't right that Herod was sleeping with his brother Philip's wife, Herodias. Herod had been scared to waste John at first 'cuz he thought John's folks would put a hurtin' on him. But on Herod's birthday, Herodias' daughter danced wildly for Herod and made him happy. When he asked her what she wanted as a reward, the little girl told him she wanted John's head on a silver platter. (Her mother had prompted her to do this 'cuz she wanted John gone—outta there.) Anyway, Herod had given his word, so he wasted brother John and gave his head to the little girl who gave it to her mother.

John's friends came and took his body and buried it. Then they went and told Jesus what had gone down. After that Herod went 'round thinking that Jesus was John come back to haunt him and he was really scared.

Jesus took off by boat to a place to be alone, but the crowd, as usual, followed Him there. Jesus was never one to turn anybody away, 'cuz when He saw them He had a lot of sympathy for them. And Jesus' boys knew Jesus had wanted to be alone, so they urged Him to send the folks away. But Jesus would have none of that.

"Nah, don't send 'em away. They traveled a long way, too. Look, give 'em something to eat."

But the brothers were kind of leery. "We ain't got nothing but five loaves of bread and two fish."

Jesus asked them to bring the bread and fish to Him. When they had, Jesus looked up to heaven and prayed. After He had blessed the food, He gave it to the brothers who gave it to the folks. And when it was all counted up, they took up twelve baskets full of food after everybody had eaten. That day more than five thousand brothers and sisters and their children had eaten.

Later, Jesus sent His boys out in a boat because He wanted to be alone. Once they were out in the middle of the sea, a big wind came and blew the boat here and there, so that Jesus got out and walked over to them on the water.

Now the brothers thought they were seeing a ghost and got scared. But Jesus calmed them down. *"Don't be scared. It's only Me,"* He told them.

And Peter called out to Jesus. "If it's You, just say the word and I'll walk out to You."

Jesus held out His hand and said, *"All right, brother Peter. Come on."*

Peter stepped out on the water on faith, keeping his eyes on Jesus. But when he looked around him and saw that the waves were high and the wind was fierce he lost his nerve. Immediately, Peter started to sink, so he cried out, "Oh, Lord. What have I done? Save me. Save me!"

Jesus walked over to him on the water and grabbed his hand. *"Oh, Peter. You've got such little faith. Here, get back in the boat."*

As soon as they got in the boat, the wind stopped. The brothers worshipped Jesus 'cuz He had to be the Almighty's son.

After they had crossed over, they came to the land of Genneesaret, where the brothers there knew who He was. That day, anybody with a bellyache was brought to Jesus. All they wanted to do was touch His clothes and be made well. And it was so that day.

Breaking The Rules

Now those wanna-be Pharisees were at it again, looking for something to diss Jesus about.

"How come your people don't wash their hands when they eat?"

And Jesus looked at them as if they had two heads. *"Why do you insist on trying to make a mountain outta a molehill? Huh? You keep stepping on the Almighty's toes because of rules that don't mean nothing to anybody but you. Look, the Almighty told you, 'give respect to your mom and dad,' saying that anybody who disses their parents should be put to death. Now you wanna say that anybody who gives himself to the church is free to diss his mother and father, so you make laws that suit you when you wanna do wrong. You're all such a bunch of hypocrites! Isaiah knew about you 'cuz your type has been 'round a long time.*

> *'These folks talk the talk, but they don't walk the walk. Their hearts are saying something totally different, so they're coming to church in vain 'cuz it don't mean a thang!'*

So this is the real deal." And He talked to the people 'cuz talking to the Pharisees was a waste of time. "*It ain't what a brother eats that make a brother bad. It's what comes outta his mouth 'cuz what he says comes from his heart.*

"*Look, every plant that ain't planted by the Almighty will be pulled up by the roots. Don't worry 'bout the Pharisees or any of these other hardheaded brothers. They are the blind trying to lead the blind. And you know that if you can't see you're liable to fall into the ditch.*"

And Peter wanted it made clearer.

"*What's up, Peter? You can't understand this when it is so simple. If you can't understand, you can see now why others who don't love the Almighty won't be able to. Okay, here's the scoop. If a man eats something, it's only a matter of time before the food he ate is passed out, but when he says something to hurt somebody, it comes from the heart. From the heart you can think 'bout killing a brother, getting down with somebody's ol' lady, or dissing the Almighty. This is what makes a brother unclean, not whether or not he washes his hands.*"

Later Jesus came to the cities of Tyre and Sidon where a Canaan sister begged Him to help her daughter who was possessed by demons.

"Help me, Lord. My daughter is really touched in the head by demons."

And Jesus didn't answer her at first, so that His boys told Him to send her away. "Look how she runs after us," they said sarcastically. "Send her away."

Jesus turned to the brothers and told them, *"I didn't come to help out brothers from Israel."* Then He turned to the woman, *"It's not good to take a little kid's food and give it to the dogs."*

But the woman answered, "Yes, sir. That's true, but even the dogs can lick up the crumbs that fall from the table."

"Sister girl, your faith is great. Your daughter is well." And with that He left and the sister's daughter was healed at that very moment.

Jesus then went to the Sea of Galilee and sat down near the mountain. And again, the people saw Him and came to Him and asked that He heal them, so He did. There were nearly four thousand folks there and after a while, Jesus asked His boys to feed the people.

"How much food we got?"

And they answered seven loaves and a few little fish. Just like before, Jesus prayed, blessed the food and fed everybody. There were even seven baskets of food left. After everybody had eaten, Jesus got into the boat and went to Magdala.

Laying A Trap

Those Pharisee brothers were always trying to get the lowdown on Jesus, so they asked Him to show them a sign from Heaven above. And this is what Jesus told them.

"Oh, yeah. You know that in the evening when the sky is red, you're gonna have good weather the next day and you know that if the sky is red in the morning, that a storm is coming. But can you read the writing on the wall about brothers today? You all are such hypocrites. You want signs and then you don't believe what you see. Well here it is in black-and-white. The only sign I'm gonna give you is the one that Jonah got in that whale." And with that said, He was gone.

When his boys had gotten Him over to the other side, they realized they didn't bring any bread. Jesus warned them, *"You need to look out. You don't want any of that stuff those bad dudes are eating."*

And they wondered if perhaps Jesus meant that they had forgotten to bring the bread, but Jesus wasn't talking about bread at all. *"Come on, guys. What's up? Don't you know I ain't talking 'bout food. Didn't you see me take a little bread and fish and feed thousands? You were there, weren't you? Nah, what I'm talking 'bout is not taking what they say to heart. Stop listenin' to what they fake in the streets."*

Finally the boys were hipped to what was really going down with Jesus.

When Jesus came to the town of Caesarea Philippi, He asked the brothers this question. *"Who do folks say I am?"*

And they answered, "Well, some say you're that brother Elijah and others say you're John the Baptist, come back from the dead. On the other hand, some even believe that you're Jeremiah or one of them other dead prophets."

Turning to Peter, Jesus asked, *"And what do you say? Who do you think I am?"*

Peter answered. "You are the Christ, Son of the Almighty, Himself!"

Then Jesus smiled. *"Right on, Peter. No brother laid this on you except My Father, the Almighty in heaven. And listen, man, 'cuz you are righteous, Peter, I will build my church on this rock and the gates of Hell can't shake it loose. You will have the keys of the Kingdom 'cuz I'll put them in your hand. Whatever is held up here on earth will be held up in heaven, but whatever is on the one on earth will be on the one in heaven."*

After He said this He told them all that they shouldn't go around telling folks He was Jesus the Christ.[20] He also told them that this was the beginning of the end 'cuz folks planned on jacking Him up real soon. Jesus let them know that the so-called head honchos were planning on wasting Him, but not to worry.

Peter, though, was having none of that. "Uh uh," he yelled. "We ain't letting that happen. Nobody's touching a hair on your head."

"Get away from me, you devil. You ain't thinking with a spiritual head. You're letting that head on your shoulder think for you instead of your heart.

"Look, I ain't said it was gonna be easy, but any brother who wants to follow Me is gonna have to suffer, too! And if you lose your life here on earth, you'll live forever in eternity with Me. What happens when a brother ends up with everything silver and gold, but loses his soul? Tell

---

[20]Jesus the Christ is also called the Messiah, the one the prophets told about hundreds of years before.

Me, how much is your soul worth? When I rise after they waste Me, I'm coming with my Father, the Almighty and giving out something worth more than gold. And I'm tellin' you, there'll be those who wished they were already dead when I come home."

Up To The Mountaintop

Six days later, Jesus went with Peter, James, and John up the mountain and right on top, Jesus changed. His face was brighter than the sun and his threads had become white like light. And standing next to him were Moses and Elijah, rapping up a storm. Peter whispered to Jesus, "It's great that we're here, sir! If you want, we could build three churches, one for you, one for Moses, and one for Elijah."

And before he finished talking, a big, bright cloud blew over and a loud voice come from the cloud. It said, *"This is my son who I love and I'm pleased with what He's doing. You need to listen to Him."*

The brothers heard this and fell on the ground, covering their faces 'cuz they were scared. But Jesus came over and pulled them up. *"Don't be afraid. Come on. Get up."*

And when they got up, they didn't see anybody but Jesus. As they headed down the mountain Jesus told them not to tell anybody what went down until He had come back from the dead.

"Look, those folks are right. Elijah had to come first to get things straight, but nobody knew who he was. He had to come before Me, the Messiah 'cuz that's the way it was written. And just like they wasted him, they're gonna waste Me. That's the way it's written."

It became clear to the brothers that Jesus was talking 'bout none other than John the Baptist.

When they got down to the bottom, the crowd was already there. A brother came running out of the crowd and fell at Jesus' feet.

"Look, man. Help my son. He's an epileptic[21] and he's always falling in the fire and water. It's dangerous. I took him to your boys, but they couldn't do nothing."

Jesus was outdone. *"Oh, spare Me these folks with so little faith. Ya'll are getting on My last nerve. Look, bring the boy to Me."*

And Jesus raised his hand and told that ol' devil to scat and the little brother was cured immediately. Later, Jesus' boys came and asked why they couldn't do that. Jesus answered, *"'Cuz you ain't got no faith. You don't believe and it don't take much. If you've got as much faith as a little tiny mustard seed, you could make a mountain move. Nothing could stand in your way."*

Later Jesus told them that His end was coming. *"It's only a matter of time before somebody stabs Me in the back and those judges waste Me for a crime I didn't commit. But three days later, I'll be up from the grave."* The brothers weren't pleased about this at all.

In Capernaum, the tax collectors asked the disciples if Jesus paid the church tax and the boys said, "Yeah." Then Peter ran in to talk to Jesus, but He already knew what had

---

[21]An epileptic is a person who has sudden convulsions or seizures.

gone down. *"Tell me, Peter. Where do the tax collectors get their money, from the hometown boys or the out of town brothers?"*

Peter said, "The out of town brothers."

"So, they really shouldn't be messing with us. But that's okay. We don't want to diss 'em. They need some money, go and catch me a fish and when you look in its mouth you'll find a dime. Drop it on the tax collector."

Floats Like A Butterfly...

"Who is the greatest in heaven?" asked the boys.

And Jesus called a little kid over to sit on His lap. He turned to the brothers and answered, *"You gotta give the Almighty His due and come to Him before you can even get in the front door. You see this kid? You wanna go to heaven? Make yourself like a child and if you don't diss this little child, you ain't dissing me.*

"But if you mess with this kid and cause him to do wrong 'cuz of what you do, it would better if they hung a concrete block 'round your neck and threw you out into the ocean. Don't you understand? You step on My toes and it's worse than death.

"Listen, my brothers. If it's the hand or foot that causes you to step outta line, cut 'em off. You'd have a better chance limping into heaven on the good foot, than not getting in at all. Hell is more than it's cracked up to be.

"If you looking in the wrong direction, go blind and set your heart on Me. It's better going one-eyed or blind than to go to hell.

"Here's a little story I like to tell. You don't want to step on My toes, boys 'cuz I've come to save folks. If a brother

has a hundred sheep and one of them goes off by hisself somewhere, does he leave the ones he's got to go and get that one?

"Yeah, he does. And I'm telling you he's happier about finding that one who went off and was found than all the others who stayed and were safe. Don't you know that the Almighty doesn't want one to get wasted and not go to heaven?

"Ya'll need to get straight with one another. If a brother makes you mad, go to him by yourself and tell him what's on your mind. Maybe you work it out and you and your brother are on the one. But if he ain't listening, then get a couple of other brothers to go with you 'cuz it is written that the truth will be heard when there are two or three people around.[22] If he still refuses to deal righteous with you, go tell the whole thing to the church. And if that don't work, let him go.

"Like I told you, whatever is held up on earth will be held up in heaven. And whatever is on the one here on earth, will be on the one with My Father. Payback has always been a monster.

"It's like this, if two or three brothers or sisters get together and ask anything, it'll happen for them. The Almighty says so. 'Cuz where two or three come together for My name's sake, I'm right there, too!"

Peter asked Jesus, "If a brother ganks me over and over again, how many times I gotta take it? Seven times?"

---

[22]See Deuteronomy, Chapter 19, verse 15. Also read about dealing with a brother who disses you in Matthew, Chapter 18, verses 15 through 17.

And Jesus said, "Brother Peter, I ain't saying seven times, but seventy times seven. It's kind of like a certain king who wanted to settle up with his employees. One of his employees owed him ten thousand dollars and he couldn't pay up, so the king wanted him evicted along with his kids and everything sold until the debt was paid. But the employee begged for mercy. 'Sir, I'm sorry, please have patience with me. I'm gonna pay you.' The king was moved and didn't really want to put the boy out, so he said, 'No problem. I forgive you.' Then, that same employee went out and found a brother who owed him a couple thousand dollars and he put his hands around his throat and demanded his money.

"'Pay up, boy or you'll be sorry.' And the brother couldn't pay and begged for mercy. The employee wasn't having none of that and had the brother arrested right there on the spot. However, other brothers who saw what went down, went and told the king everything. 'You wouldn't believe how he treated that guy over a little bit of money.' The king was really miffed. He called the employee to him.

"'You are really something! How dare you treat somebody like this after I've given you a second chance.' He fired the brother on the spot and had the same thing done to him that he did to the little brother down the street.

"Now here's what I'm saying to you. If you can't forgive one another, how you gonna expect the Almighty to forgive you?"

D-I-V-O-R-C-E Doesn't Spell Relief

Jesus finished up in Galilee and went back to Judea, right across from the Jordan River. As always, brothers and sisters followed Him and begged Him to heal their sick. But behind them were those swoll-headed Pharisees, looking for a way to trap Jesus into saying something that would discredit Him.

"Hey, man. Do you think divorce is all right?"

"Nah, it ain't right. In the beginning the Almighty made a brother and a sister and told 'em to join together as one. A brother leaves his mother and goes to his wife, and no brother can destroy what the Almighty has put together."

"Okay, if that's true, why did Moses let folks divorce each other?"

Jesus told them. *"Moses was tired of you guys clowning him over everything he told you not to do, so he gave you some slack, that's why. But I'm here to set the record straight. Divorcing your wife is a no-no, except should she be jocking another brother. And if a brother marries a sister who has divorced her husband, it's still the same sin."*

And His boys agreed that if a brother wasn't going to stay with his wife, it was better he didn't get married at all.

"Now you know everybody ain't buying that. You just have to trust that the Almighty will show you the way. Look some are born and can't get married 'cuz they don't have the right equipment, some 'cuz they've been cut on by men and some don't marry 'cuz they want to devote their time to the Almighty. I say whoever can deal with it should."

Later a couple of parents brought their kids 'round for Jesus to bless them. And His boys thought it was best not to bother their master and sent them away. Jesus wasn't happy about it and told them, *"Look, let these kids alone. They're welcome anytime and nobody should stand in their way."* Then He held His hand out and blessed each child.

A man came to Jesus later that day and asked, "Good brother, tell me. What should I do to have eternal life?"

"You wanna go to heaven? Follow the Almighty's program, it's that simple. And by the way, thanks for calling me good 'cuz you're really making that call on the Almighty. He deserves it."

"But what's His program all about?" the brother asked.

"You know. Don't kill. Don't mess with somebody else's ol' lady or ol' man. Don't steal. Be on the one with your parents and love your next-door neighbor like you'd wanna be loved."

"That's cool. I've done that. Now what."

"Now give up everything you got and follow me."

The young brother hung his head 'cuz he had lots of money and didn't want to give it up.

Jesus turned to His boys and said, *"You see? It'd be easier for a big ol' camel to try and squeeze through the eye of a needle than a fat cat to get into heaven."*

"So, then it's a waste of time to try and get saved?"

"It would be if it weren't for the Almighty. He's got a plan that will make this road a lot easier to travel."

"Okay," said Peter. "We've given up everything. What's in it for us?"

Jesus smiled and looked at Peter. *"One day I'm gonna sit on a throne and everybody's gonna know that I am the one. When that happens, I'll judge every soul and those who gave it up for Me will be rewarded a 100 times over and live forever. But here's the kicker, my brother Peter. Some of those who were first to try this thing might be last getting in, and those last just might be first."*

Working Hard For The Money

"I don't know how I can make things much plainer," Jesus told His folks. *"The Almighty's kingdom is kinda like a big landowner who goes out and hires a couple of brothers to do some work in the vineyard for 'bout $20 a day. A few hours later he saw some brothers standing 'round doing nothing, so he offered them a job too, tellin 'em, 'whatever you think is fair, I'll pay.' About six hours later, he ran up on some brothers and did the same thing. When the day was almost over, he ran into some more brothers and offered them a gig and even after eleven hours he saw other brothers standing there doing nothing and asked them to work, too.*

"That night, the employer came 'round to see what was happening and told the supervisors, 'Tell 'em it's quitting time and pay them. Call the last ones first and pay 'em $20.'

"Now when the guys who started work early that morning got their pay, it was the same even though they wanted more. And the brothers were bent out of shape wanting to know why they had been cheated. The owner of the vineyard heard them and asked, 'What's up? Didn't

you agree to work for $20? So, what's your problem? I can pay folks whatever I want. It's my money.'

"*And that's why I tell you about folks being first and last. Look, a lot folks are called, but ain't many chosen.*"

Later, on their way to Jerusalem, Jesus told them, "*It won't be long before somebody stabs Me in the back and then I'll be wasted. Before I die lots of brothers will be making fun and making it hard on Me, but on the third day, I'm coming back.*"

Now James' and John's mom wanted to ask Jesus a favor. "Can my boys sit to the right and left of You when You get to this heavenly place?"

Jesus shook His head. "*You don't know what you're asking Me, ma'am. You think your boys can handle what's going down? You think they can die with Me?*"

And the brothers answered, "Yeah, we think we can."

So Jesus replied. "*All right, 'cuz if you say so you'll have to deal with everything I'm dealing with. But here's the clincher. I can't give you the place to the right or left of Me. That choice belongs to the Almighty and you gotta earn it.*"

But the others were jealous that John and James even asked. Jesus told them to cool it. "*We ain't like those politicians who sell favors for titles. I'm telling you that anybody that wants to take on being a leader gotta know he's gonna be a servant to you. You can't lead if you can't follow. Don't you know I didn't come to run things, but to be of service to others?*"

Shortly thereafter, they left Jericho and were followed by the crowds again. Two blind men accosted them on the road and begged, "Oh, Lord, Son of David, have mercy, man!" Jesus stood there for a moment before asking, *"What you want?"*

And the brothers asked Jesus to let them see. In a flash, their sight came back. Nobody could stop them from following Jesus after that.

He'll Be Coming Round The Mountain

The brothers and Jesus were coming close to Jerusalem as they went through Bethphage, at the Mount of Olives. Jesus sent the boys ahead, telling them, *"When you get into town, you'll see a donkey and a horse tied up. Bring them to Me and if anybody bothers you, tell 'em 'The Lord wants 'em,' and they'll let them go. No problem."*

And it was just like the prophet Zechariah said a long time ago, "Tell the Zion sister that the King is on his way riding a donkey. And he ain't got the big head about it."[23]

Of course it was just like Jesus said it would be, so they brought the animals, covered them and Jesus sat astride them. And the crowd roared when He came into town, yelling "Bless the Son of David 'cuz He's finally come."

A lot of folks didn't know who He was and asked those cheering, "What's going on? Who is that brother?" They told them, "Doncha know? That's Jesus, the brother from Nazareth, near Galilee."

When Jesus got inside the town, He went straight to the church there. Seated 'round tables were brothers selling their stuff with cash registers everywhere. It made Jesus

---

[23]See Zachariah, Chapter 9, verse 9.

mad and He clowned those brothers something fierce, turning over their tables and telling them to get out.

"Ya'll get out now. This is a church for prayer and service to the Almighty and you've made it a house for thieves. Get out!"

After Jesus had cleaned up the place, the sick and infirmed came to visit and Jesus made them well again. And the preachers who had allowed such foolishness were mad at Jesus now, 'cuz they heard the crowd outside yelling, "Hosannah to the Son of David." They were excited 'bout the Son of the Almighty being 'round and that changes had been made. And Jesus knowing what those head honchos were thinking, said, *"You got that? Outta the mouths of little babies and infants barely able to talk, folks are ready for the real deal."*

Jesus soon left there and went to Bethany where He spent the night. In the morning He was hungry and saw a fig tree over 'cross the way. But when He got there the fig tree didn't have fruit, so He told the tree, *"No fruit will grow on you—ever!"* The fig tree shriveled up and died. The boys were amazed.

"How'd you do that?"

"That ain't nothing. With faith you can tell a mountain, 'go into the ocean,' and it'll happen. Anything you ask in prayer, believing that it'll happen, will happen."

Those big time preachers and politicians wanted Jesus' hide bad. They tried to trap him. "Hey, what gives you the right to do these things? How dare you come and try and tell us what to do?"

"You wanna know, don't you? Well, I'll tell you if you can tell Me how John had the right to do what He did? Was it from brothers, like yourself, or the Almighty, Hisself?"

And the brothers sat and thought a minute 'cuz if they said, "From heaven," Jesus would ask them why they didn't believe John, and if they said, "From men," the folks in this town would think brother John had been a prophet after all. Finally they decided they would just say they didn't know.

"That's what I thought. So I ain't telling you nothing either."

Then He broke it down to them this way by telling them a story.

"A brother had two sons and went to one and said, 'Go and mow the yard,' and the brother didn't want to and said. 'Nah, Pop.' A few minutes later he felt bad, so he went back to his dad and apologized and went out and mowed the grass. The next time he went to his other son and asked him to mow the yard, and the boy said, 'No problem, Dad,' but he didn't do it, even though he promised he would.

"Now tell me, which son did what his father wanted?"

And they answered, "The first little brother, of course."

"All right then. Them pimps and whores you put down will get to the Almighty 'fore you will 'cuz they believed. Even after you saw what was going down, you didn't do nothing but blow hot smoke. Get it?

"Okay, let Me break it down further. There was a certain brother who owned some land where he planted some grapes and then built a wall around it. He also built

a winepress and a tower and rented it to folks who would work the land and bring his grapes in when they were ready. And when it was time to bring in the grapes, he sent folks to bring them to him. But the folks he rented the place to killed one of them and threw rocks at the others. Over and over again, the brother sent folks to try and get his grapes, but they just kept wasting anybody who came. Finally, the brother sent his only son, and you know what? They killed him, too. Now it won't be long before the owner has to come to claim his property. What do you think he'll do to those guys?"

"He'll waste those brothers, that's what. Then he'll hire somebody else."

"Don't you guys read? It says in the Word that 'The stone that the builders threw to the side has become the main stone. This was the Almighty's plan all 'long and ain't it grand.'[24] *So here's what I say to you. The Almighty's kingdom will be taken away from you and given to those who will take care of it."*

And those big time preachers and politicians got a little antsy thinking that Jesus was talking 'bout them. They didn't like it, so they plotted and planned to waste Jesus at the first opportunity.

I'm Getting Married In The Morning

Jesus was hipped to what these politico and preacher guys were thinking so he told them another story. *"The Almighty's kingdom is like a certain king who decided it was time his son got married and he told his people that*

---

[24]Read Psalm 118, verses 22 and 23.

they needed to send out invitations to this big wedding. Folks didn't rsvp or nothing else, 'cuz they didn't want to come. So he hired somebody to invite the folks and told them to let the people know that this wedding would be kicking with fine food and drink. 'Ask 'em to come, please,' the brother said.

"Again the folks made fun and said, nah, they weren't coming and the folks who had been hired to make the wedding arrangements were wasted outta spite. The brother was hurt 'cuz none of his so-called friends wanted to come, so he said to his employees, 'I don't care who comes, get total strangers 'cuz this wedding feast is the lick.' Soon, the brothers house was full of people good and bad having a good time. Then the boss came and saw that one of the guests wasn't dressed properly so he had his boys tie him up and get him outta there. And there was great pain behind this.

When Jesus had said all this, the Pharisee brothers plotted revenge. They wanted to off Jesus 'cuz He was speaking the truth and they didn't like what they were hearing. So they sent some of King Herod's boys and had them ask, "Hey, teach, you're wise and all that, and do what the Almighty tells you to do; so tell us. We know you ain't got respect for no one person, so should we pay taxes to Caesar?"

"'What's with you guys? You think I don't see through you? Show Me a gold coin." And when they had done this, He turned it over and handed it back to them. *"Whose face is on this money and what does it say?"*

"It's Caesar's pic, man, and his name."

"All right then. Give up what's Caesar's to Caesar. And whatever belongs to the Almighty, give it up to God."

The boys were amazed. They had hope to trap Him, but what He said made sense, so they left Him alone.

Next came those Sadducee brothers who didn't believe anybody could be raised from the dead, so they came to test Him, too. "Teacher, ol' man Moses said that if a man dies and has no kids, his brother is supposed to get down with his ol' lady so the brother will have a kid with his name. Now, uh, I got seven brothers. Okay? And the first brother died without having any kids so the second brother married her, but he died, too. And seven brothers died and finally so did the sister. No kids, now, from anybody. Got that? Here's the question. When they're raised from the dead, whose ol' lady she gonna be?"

"Ya'll ain't even smart. You don't know the Word and you don't know God! When we are resurrected, brought back to eternal life, we don't worry 'bout the everyday, flesh to flesh thing. Won't be no need. You'll be like the angels and wanna know something else? The Almighty is the power behind Abraham, behind Isaac and Jacob. He's the God of the living, fool, not of the dead!"

Now when the Pharisees heard that Jesus had ranked heavy on the Sadducees, they got together again to try and trip Him up. A lawyer decided he was man enough to put Jesus to the test, and asked Him, "What's the greatest rule?"

"Love the Almighty with your complete heart, soul and mind. It's the first rule and the greatest rule. And the second one is love your brothers and sisters like you

wanna be loved. These two go hand in hand, my dear legal mind. It's everything in the end that the big rule and the preachers talk about."

Later Jesus asked how King David could possibly be His dad. *"How can you call me Son of David when David himself said, 'The Lord said to My Lord, sit on the right here 'til the folks that been dissing you are something to put your feet on.' If David calls me Lord, how am I his son?"*

And they didn't know 'cuz it was a puzzle. After this they didn't dare ask Him any questions.

Coming Down Hard on Some Wanna-be Brothers

Jesus knew that folks were plotting His demise and that it was only a matter of time before they got their wish. Only He wanted to go on record with the truth.

"You know these highfalutin leaders sat right down at Moses' feet while he did his thing. And what they did was give more grief than was necessary to poor folks trying to get their act together. They've got that 'do what I say, not what I do attitude.' More, they don't even try to let folks know what's going down. Their whole act is to be seen so they can showboat.

"Yeah, they think that keeping their image intact is more important than doing what is right and compassionate. You see them in the best restaurants, at the best hotels, throwing money 'round like they're somebody. 'I'm Reverend So-and-so,' they say walking 'round like peacocks.

"But the Almighty is the real teacher. Don't fall for the lies of these wanna-be brothers. Don't call Me Father, 'cuz the Almighty is the One. These folks wanna be respected, then I say let 'em serve the people. 'Cuz those folks who think they're so high and mighty 'bout themselves will be nothing in the end. And those folks who put on the jacket of humility will be raised up in the end.

"You Pharisees and preachers are such hypocrites. You make it hard for brothers to come to the Almighty. You take and take and take. All you're doing is buying yourself a one-way ticket to hell. The pomp and circumstance, this circus you call worship, don't mean nothing to Him. You make the tradition greater than the Almighty. You put on a show, but inside is an utter mess. You look like you are doing the right thing, but your heart is black. You build fine churches and put in fine furniture, but you don't know what's up. You're pitiful, I tell you, pitiful.

"The Almighty has been sending folks[25] to try and tell you 'bout what is right and how to straighten your lives out, but you don't listen. You never have and looks like you never will. And you wasted one of those very brothers who came to tell you the truth. Remember brother Zachariah? You killed him 'cuz you didn't wanna hear it. You knew he told the truth. But don't worry, your time is coming.

"Brothers of Jerusalem, who wanna be so great. You're murders of prophets and a stone 'round My neck. The

---

[25]The Almighty sent several preachers and teachers to warn people about talking out of both sides of their mouth. They were called prophets and included brothers like Isaiah, Jeremiah, Zachariah and a host of others. Review the Old Testament for a list of the prophets.

Almighty tried to tell you what was right. He tried to bring you under his wing kinda like a hen with her chicks, but you kept on dissing Him. But enjoy what's left, 'cuz you won't hear from Me again until you say, 'God bless Him who comes in the name of the Lord.'"

No Stone Unturned

After Jesus said what He had to say, He left and took His boys to see the church. Jesus told them, *"You see these things? It's all gonna come tumbling down, one stone at a time."*

He went and sat down on the Mount of Olives. His disciples came to talk to Him on the q.t. "We wanna ask you a question. When is all this coming down?"

"Don't be fooled. A whole lot of folks gonna be telling you they're down with the right information. They'll tell you 'bout wars, but they don't know nothing. This is how you will know when it's about to come down.

"Nations will come up against each other. So will kingdoms against other kingdoms. There will be folks dying with no food and water by the hundreds. There will be diseases that can't be cured and the world will literally be shaken apart in some places. And this is only the beginning.

"Men will make life miserable for those who try and do the right thing. And they will hate you for what you do. Whole bunches of fake preachers will try and tell you they got the answer, but you'll know the truth in your heart. It ain't about those who think they know the answers, it's about those who go the distance.

"I'm saying this now, so the world will know I talked 'bout it long before it happened. And when these things go down like Daniel of a long time ago talked about,[26] ya'll better run to them hills. Those on top of the house, should stay put and those who are out in the field, don't worry 'bout packing a suitcase. When this comes down, you better be ready or you'll find yourself left. It'll be sad for nursing mommas and their babies. And one should hope that it doesn't come down in the winter or on a Sunday 'cuz it'll be hell to pay for those who wanna be on the one with the Almighty. Folks will be stabbing you in the back and calling you names. Worse, they'll want to waste you for what you believe.

"And when the screaming and yelling has stopped, it'll grow dark. This will be the signal that I'm comin' back. From all 'round the world, folks need only look up in the sky and there I'll be floating down on a cloud. Heavy, ain't it? There will be horns blowing better than Dizzy, and My people, the ones who never gave up, will be raised up in glory.

"Remember the fig tree? You know when summer is coming 'cuz of the way her branch looks. It's the same way with My coming. Those that know Me, will know the signs.

"And heaven and earth as you know will be no more. But My word, it's gonna stay. Only thing is, only Me and My Father know the day and the hour.

---

[26]See Daniel, Chapter 11, verse 31; and Chapter 12, verses 11-12.

"It'll be just like before the flood.[27]   *Folks partied up until the first raindrops fell, and when it kept on raining, they were caught with their pants down. So, all I can tell you is stay on the one with the Almighty 'cuz you don't know when He's coming. He's gonna peep and creep, and unless you've been doing what is right and good, He'll be like the thief who comes when you ain't prepared.*

"So, are you wise? You got your stuff together? Or are you bad and saying to yourself, 'The Almighty ain't doing nothing. He ain't going nowhere?' You decide 'cuz it really is in your hand."

Hold On, I'm Coming

Jesus continued to break down how things were gonna go down by telling them stories. And one story went like this:

"There were ten sisters who took their lamps and went to meet their ol' man. Five of the sisters were smart and five of 'em were silly. The silly sisters took their lamps, but didn't take a lot a oil. The wise sisters took their lamps and some extra oil just in case. The ol' man was late, 'cuz something had kept him away, so the sisters lay down to sleep for a spell. When they awakened, somebody was yelling, 'Everybody get up. The ol' man is here. Get up.'

"And they were all in a frenzy trying to get ready, but the silly girls didn't have enough oil. They begged the other five sisters to share, but the sisters said, 'Uh uh.

---

[27]Jesus is talking about the flood where God saved only Noah and his family along with the pairs of animals.

Might not be enough for us. You best find someone to sell you some more.' So, the sisters ran out to try and find some oil, but while they were out, the ol' man came and took everybody to the wedding. When the wedding started, the attendants closed and locked the doors.

"Well, those silly girls came running all out of breath with the oil they bought, but it was already too late. The door was shut and they were locked out.

"Know what this story means? Better be prepared 'cuz you don't know when He's coming."

And to break it down further, He told this story.

"A brother got ready to go on a long trip and he called his people together and gave 'em money to work with while he was gone. To one he gave 'bout $5,000, to another 'bout two grand, and another one grand. After he left, the first two brothers went to work building up their nest eggs, but the brother with only one grand took his dough and buried it out in the backyard. Soon the boss returned and asked about his money. The brother with five grand had made a whopping ten grand, and the other brother doubled his money as well. To each of these brothers, the boss said, 'Good job,' but when the brother turned to the guy he'd given the grand, the brother stammered and hung his head. 'Uh, look, here's your grand. I didn't want no mess 'bout your money and if I lost it you'd be mad, so I didn't do nothing with it 'cuz I wasn't risking my neck. Anyways,' the silly brother said, 'you're always taking what you ain't worked for, so here's your money.'

"Well, the boss was really sore. He told the brother he was a lazy, good for nothing boy. 'Instead of burying it, you could've at least put in a savings account to earn some

interest, but no, you go and let it rot underground.' He took
the money and handed it to the brother with ten grand.
'Here! When you learn to do with a little, you'll be able to
handle a lot. But if you ain't down with even the smallest
task, how'd you expect to get the big job.'

"And one day I'll be back dressed to the nines," Jesus
told them. "And when that happens, those folks who did
with the little will get theirs. And that's the way I'm
gonna know who is who 'cuz of those that did right. Those
that ain't worth a hill of beans will be discarded. Wait and
see. I'll ask folks a couple of simple questions and they
won't be able to answer. I'll say, 'When I was hungry did
you feed Me? When I was thirsty, did you give Me
something to drink? Did you put clothes on My back when
I didn't have no rags?' And those wanna-be brothers will
be saying, 'I didn't see you naked.' 'I didn't see you hungry
or thirsty.' 'What are you talking 'bout?' Then I'll know
who's righteous and who isn't. I'll tell those wanna-be
brothers, trying to get into heaven with Me, 'Get away
from Me 'cuz you ain't nothing to Me.' I'm telling you, you
do this to the lowest of the low and you do it also to Me.
And the punishment for dissing My brothers on earth is
hell to pay, I promise."

Plotting The Driveby

Jesus knew they wanted to waste Him, so he tried to get
His boys up for the occasion.

"In a couple of days, after the Passover,[28] *I'm gonna be taken to jail to be tried and then wasted."*

Around this time, the big time preachers and teachers, and leaders of the people got together at the house of the biggest preacher in town whose name was Caiaphas. "We gotta get rid of Him," they plotted.

"But not before the feast is over with 'cuz folks will be bent outta shape over dissing the Almighty's feast," somebody else said. "We gotta do this right. We want folks to be behind us on this."

When Jesus came to Bethany He went to Simon's house (Simon was a leper) and a sister came up to Jesus and poured some expensive, sweet smelling oil on his head. The disciples were mad.

"How dare she do something silly like that? That was expensive stuff. We coulda used it for cash and given it to the poor."

But Jesus shushed them. *"Don't bother the sister. She's just getting My body ready for My funeral. Anyway, I'm not gonna be 'round here long. It's okay. What the sister has done will be remembered forever."*

One of Jesus' twelve boys went to see the preachers. His name was Judas Iscariot and he asked the preachers, "Whata you give me for Jesus?"

And they counted up thirty pieces of silver so that the plot was hatched. Judas was to turn in Jesus.

The time had come and it was the first day of the Feast of Passover, so the boys wanted to know how Jesus wanted

---

[28]Passover was a day of celebration which helped many remember that the angels of the Almighty had passed over the children of Israel and saved them from death.

to celebrate. And Jesus told them, *"Go into town and see this brother. Tell him that your teacher wants to celebrate dinner at his house."*

The Last Supper

Jesus and his disciples sat 'round the table eating and drinking according to the way the Feast was done up. Things were pretty quiet until Jesus told them, *"One of you will betray Me."*

And everybody, including Judas, asked if he was the one. Jesus told Judas, *"Remember, you said it."* Jesus then took bread and broke it up, handing some to everybody.

"Take this and eat it 'cuz this is My body."

Then He took some wine and blessed it before handing it over to each of the boys. *"Drink, this is My blood. This means that we've got a pack, a deal—that I'm dying 'cuz of you so that things will be right between folks and the Almighty. This is the last time I'm drinking 'til I come back and drink again with each of you."*

Then He told them, *"After tonight everybody's gonna scatter to the wind, 'cuz it was written that when the big boys bring Me down, you all will scatter.*[29] *But when I come back after three days, you'll see Me in Galilee."*

But Peter was positive that even if everything went down like Jesus said, he, Peter, would stand and fight for Him. Jesus shook his head. *"Peter. Peter. Peter. I'm tellin' you as sure as My name is Jesus, before the rooster crows, you'll tell folks you never even knew Me. You'll do it three times."*

---

[29]See Zachariah, Chapter 13, verse 7.

Peter was adamant. "No I won't. I'll die with you. I'm not gonna diss you that way." Everybody else said the same thing.

After dinner, Jesus and the disciples went up to a place called Gethsemane and Jesus asked the boys to wait over on the other side while He went up to pray. He took Peter, James and John with Him.

"Ya'll don't know. This is a terrible burden and I've got some mighty powerful praying to do. Stay here and watch with Me."

So, Jesus went up to say His prayers. He fell on His face and called up to the Almighty. *"Father, I wish it were possible not to have to go through with this, but whatever You want done, that's the way it's gonna be."*

Later when Jesus finished praying He walked over to the brothers and they were fast asleep. *"What's the matter? You can't stay up one hour? Come on, watch and pray with Me or you might be tempted to do something wrong. I know your spirit is willing. Why must your flesh be so weak?"*

He went up again and started praying. When He took a break a second time, He found the brothers asleep again. And He did this a third time, and He still came down to find the brothers cutting some Zs.

"You guys are pitiful. It's time and you've slept most of our time away. Come on. Let's get this over with."

While He spoke about these things to His boys, Judas came over with a bunch of brothers carrying weapons. These brothers worked for the big-time preachers in town, and Judas told them, "Whoever I kiss on the cheek, take

Him. He's yours." He then walked up to Jesus and said, "Hey, Teacher," and kissed Him.

Jesus asked Judas, *"What's up yourself, Judas?"*

Then the police came and started to take Jesus away when one of the brothers with Jesus took out his sword and cut off the ear of the brother holding him.

"You live by the sword, you die by the sword. Put it away. Don't you know I could get out of this if I wanted. My Father is more powerful than steel. It's gotta be this way 'cuz that's what was told a long time ago. You didn't have to do it this way, sneaking 'round in the dark. I sat in the broad daylight and you didn't touch Me, you cowards. This was done 'cuz that's what the Almighty told the prophets." And then just like Jesus had said, the disciples took off in every direction.

So the police took Jesus to stand before Rev. Caiaphas. The other bad honchos were there, too. Peter followed and lay low, trying to see what was going down.

Now inside the brothers tried to find an excuse for wasting Jesus. They asked folks to testify against Him, but found nobody willing to do it. Finally, they found two liars to testify against Jesus.

"Yep, He's the one," the brother was saying. "I heard Him say that He could destroy the church of the Almighty and put it back together again in three days."

The preacher looked over at Jesus. "Got anything to say?"

Jesus said nothing to these trumped-up charges. So the preacher got frustrated and asked Him, "Just tell us. Are you the living Almighty? Are you the Christ, the Son of the Almighty?"

"It's just like that. One day you'll see this Son of the Almighty coming on a cloud with all the power."

So then the preacher went, "Ah ha! I got you! This is blasphemy. What more proof do you need? He deserves to die."

And murmuring like you never heard went up. "Yeah, waste the brother." Then they spit on Him and hit Him, mocking Him to tell them, "Which one of us did it, you know so much?"

Outside Peter sat around trying to listen to what was going down, but couldn't hear anything. A young sister saw him, and yelled to everybody, "He was with this Jesus of Galilee."

Peter shook his head. "Uh uh. I don't know what you're talking 'bout." He hung his head and tried to slide away.

"Yeah. Yeah, you are. I saw you," said another sister.

"Hush. You don't know what you're talking 'bout."

Then a brother agreed. "You're right. He was with Jesus."

Peter was outdone. He yelled at them. "I don't know this Jesus. Why do you keep saying that?" Immediately a rooster crowed and Peter felt lower than low. He remembered that Jesus had said, *"Before the rooster crows, you'll say three times you never knew Me."* Peter sat down and cried his heart out 'cuz what Jesus said was true. He had denied Christ.

Face Off With The Governor

That morning, the preachers took Jesus, bound and gagged, over to Governor Pilate, asking him to figure out a way to waste Jesus according to the law.

In the meantime, Judas felt bad for stabbing Jesus in the back. In fact, he took the money and brought it back to the preachers. "Take it. Jesus is innocent. I shouldn't have done this."

But the preachers only scoffed at him. "That ain't got nothing to do with us. Take your money and go."

Judas threw down the money and left the church feeling worse than before. He went out to the nearest tree and hung himself. The preachers looked at the money on the floor and decided it wouldn't be in their best interest to put the money back in their account; instead they bought a cemetery to bury strangers. To this day the cemetery is called the "Field of Blood" 'cuz Jeremiah the prophet had said long ago, "They took thirty pieces of silver which was the blood money used to betray Jesus, and bought a graveyard."[30]

Jesus stood before the governor, Pontius Pilate.

"Are you king of the Jews," he asked Jesus.

"You said it."

The preachers started yelling accusations back and forth, but Jesus didn't say nothing to them. So, Pilate asked Him, "Why don't you defend yourself, man?"

Jesus said nothing.

Once a year Pilate usually did an early release of one prisoner at the citizens' request, so he asked the folks this question. "Who do you want released? Jesus or this murderer Barabbas?" He knew that the preachers were just jealous of Jesus, and he really didn't wanna have

---

[30]See Jeremiah, Chapter 32, Verses 6 through 9.

anything to do with this mockery or the trumped-up charges. He tried to figure a way out of it.

His wife, who was sitting next to him, leaned over and said, "Don't do nothing to this brother, honey. I'm telling you, I've been dreaming and it ain't right what they're doing." And Pilate thought the folks would want Jesus, but the preachers had campaigned against Him, so they asked for Barabbas.

Then Pilate asked, "What am I gonna do with Jesus?"

And the crowd yelled, "Waste the dude. Waste him!"

Pilate wanted to know what Jesus had done, but they only yelled that they wanted His blood and Pilate was one of those politicians who liked his job, so he did as they asked. He gave Barabbas early release and sent Jesus to His death.

Jesus was taken down to the gallows where the soldiers made fun of Him. They dressed Him in a red robe and put a crown of thorns on His head. In His hand they put a reed and pretended to bow down before Him.

"Hey, King Jesus. What's up, man?"

And it was on. They spit on Him and pushed and shoved Him. They beat Him upside the head and cursed Him, too. After they had big fun, they took Jesus out to kill Him.

They made Jesus carry the cross they were going to hang Him on, but He stumbled, so they got a brother named Simon to carry His cross. Simon carried that cross up to Golgotha (which means Place of the Skull) and put it down. Then the soldiers gave Jesus some wine to drink mixed with something bitter, but He didn't want any of it.

Last they nailed Him on a cross. They took His clothes and gambled for them.[31]

The soldiers were told to keep a watch over Jesus 'cuz they wanted to make sure He was dead. Over His head, the soldiers hung a sign which said, 'This is Jesus, King of the Jews.' On either side of Jesus they also nailed two robbers to crosses.

The crowd gathered at the foot of the hill and mocked Jesus. "Hey, Jesus. So, you're gonna tear down the church and build it up in three days. Well, you so bad. Save yourself." Others said, "Get down off that cross. You so mighty, so you say." Then they turned to each other. "Hah! He ain't so tough. He can't even save himself."

The robbers even felt that this wasn't the king.

After about six hours, it started to get dark. All the way 'til the ninth hour, when Jesus cried, *"Eli, Eli, lama sabachthani?"* What He was saying was, *"Almighty Father, why have you given up on Me?"*

And the folks thought He was calling to Elijah to come and save Him, so they gave Him some bad tasting wine. But the others were full of themselves and said, "Oh, yeah. Right. Let him call Elijah. See if he comes."

Jesus said it one more time and then He died. And right then and there, the curtain hanging in the Temple was torn in two from top to bottom, the earth shook something fierce, and even the rocks split. Graves opened and bodies of some of the saints were raised to life. Lots of folks saw them.

---

[31]The prophecy about gambling for Jesus' clothes can be found in Psalm 22, verse 18.

Those soldiers told to watch over Jesus took off like a light, yelling, "Oh, He really is the Son of the Almighty."

Over on the other side, watching everything was Mary Magdalene, and James and John's mom, Mary.

That night a very rich man from the city of Arimathea whose name was Joseph went to Pilate and begged for Jesus' body. Pilate didn't care. He told the man he could have it.

And Joseph took the body and wrapped it in a linen cloth and put it in a grave which he had dug out of solid rock. After they laid Him inside, a big ol' rock was rolled in front. Mary Magdalene and Mary sat on opposite sides of the rock.

The next day the preachers came to Pilate and asked his indulgence. "Remember, this brother said He'd rise in three days? While we don't believe it, we don't want nobody stealing the body and saying, 'He rose,' when we know he can't. People might believe it."

Pilate didn't care. "You got a guard. Go ahead. Do what you want."

They went to the grave and secured it by sealing the stone and placing a guard over it.

A King Is Risen

On Sunday, near dawn, Mary Magdalene and Mary went to the grave to visit. While they were standing there, the earth shook, splitting open and an angel from heaven come down and moved away the stone. The angel was so bright it was breathtaking. His threads were whiter than snow. It spooked the stuffings out of the guards so that they fainted like dead men.

The angel spoke calmly to the two sisters. "Hey, don't go getting yourself outta whack, 'cuz I know you came to see Jesus, but He ain't here. No, ma'am. He's risen just like He said He would." And he took the sisters into the grave and showed them where He used to be, but wasn't there no more.

"Listen," the angel to the women. "Run, don't walk, to tell the others that Jesus Christ has beaten death. He's on His way to Galilee and if you wanna see Him that's where you gotta go."

The sisters were overjoyed and took off to tell the story. Just as they turned the corner to tell the great news, none other than Jesus met them, saying, *"Rejoice, sisters!"* The sisters fell to their knees and worshipped Jesus. They were real glad to see Him.

Then Jesus said to them, *"Go on and tell the brothers to go on to Galilee. That's where I'll be."*

The guards in the meantime, had come to and ran to tell the preachers and others that what Jesus said was true. He wasn't jocking nobody. The brother knew His stuff. The preachers were scared that the folks would find out the truth, so they laid a bunch of change on the guards and told them to tell nobody what had happened. "And look, my brothers, we'll clear things with the Governor for you. We'll tell him that those followers of His came and stole Him." The guards didn't care. They took the money and ran and the gossip was that Jesus' boys had come and taken Him away in the night.

Later eleven of those followers met Jesus in Galilee near the mountain and when they saw Him, they fell down on their faces and worshipped Him. Jesus spoke.

"I've got the power. I now run heaven and earth 'cuz through the Almighty I beat death and sin. Go and baptize others, preach and teach to all nations, and watch. I've been telling you to watch and pray 'cuz I'm coming again. But I want you to know one thing, that even though you won't see Me, I'll be with you to the very end." Amen.

The end of the Book of Matthew.
May the Almighty bless the reading of His Word!

The Word According to Mark

Mark was a friend of the Apostle Paul (who doesn't come on the scene until after Jesus rises from the dead) and he wrote these particular chapters to show that Jesus came to serve humankind.

Paving The Road to Glory

Long time ago a prophet named Isaiah told folks that a little brother would be born and lead the people back to the Almighty, but not before some brutal, wanna-be brothers would waste Him. Then He could rise from the dead and show the world how much the Almighty really loved folks. This little brother would be the Almighty's very own Son.

Now after Jesus came (nobody knew who He was except maybe His momma), there was this wild brother named John the Baptist who went 'round and preached that brothers needed to start doing right and come back to the Almighty. And when a brother confessed that he was sinful, John would baptize him. As he did so, he'd tell him, "I baptize you with water, but soon there's a brother so tough, He'll baptize you with the Holy Spirit."

One day it happened. Jesus came from Nazareth of Galilee and asked John to baptize Him in the Jordan River. And when Jesus came up outta that water, the heavens opened up and the Spirit of the Almighty came down light like a dove. A voice from Heaven said softly, *"You are my Son who I love and I'm pleased."*

The Spirit was powerful. It drove Jesus straight into the wilderness where He fasted for forty days and then was tempted by that ol' devil, hisself. He told that ol' devil to "git" and he did. Then the angels of the Almighty came down and took care of Him.

John, on the other hand, was put in prison 'cuz some folks just didn't like what he was saying, so they trumped up some charges and threw him behind bars. Jesus knew that this was His cue, so He said, *"It's time. Let's roll 'cuz the Almighty's Kingdom is come. Repent. It's time to give up your evil ways and believe in the Almighty again."*

Walking long the shores by the Sea of Galilee, Jesus ran into two brothers named Andrew and Simon, who was later called Peter. *"Follow Me, My brothers, and you will be fishers of men."* No hesitation, the brothers dropped what they were doing and followed Jesus. On down the road, He ran into James and John who were brothers and the sons of Zebedee. Once Jesus gave the word, they, too, followed Him.

Further down, they sat inside the church in Capernaum and there Jesus rapped with the brothers, teaching them of the kingdom of heaven. Every brother there had his mouth wide open 'cuz what He taught was awesome.

Now there was a brother inside the church who was filled with a terrible spirit, and that bad ol' spirit saw Jesus and knew exactly who He was. "Hey, man, don't bother us. We ain't got nothing to do with you. You wanna waste us. We know who you are, Holy brother of the Almighty."

But Jesus was having none of it. *"Uh uh, you unclean spirit. You gotta come outta there."* And as quick as that, the spirit threw the brother around a bit, but it had to come out. The brothers 'round the church were amazed. Who was this brother, they asked themselves, who could order a spirit around?

Later that day, Jesus and the brothers came outta church and went to have dinner at Peter's house where they found out that his mother-in-law was sick with fever.

With just a word, Jesus touched the sister and soon she was up cooking and fussing over them like nothing was wrong.

The next morning, early before the sun rose, Jesus went outside to pray. And His boys went looking for Him and once they found Him, they told Him that everybody was looking for Him.

"Yeah, I know. Let's go over to the next town so I can preach to the brothers. This is the reason I'm here." He preached in and outta churches all over the place and when it was necessary, put a hurting on a bad spirit so that it had to leave.

In one of the towns, a brother with the leper's disease begged Jesus to clean him up. Jesus was touched that the brother believed and told him, *"No problem."* And just like that it was done. He told the brother afterwards not to tell anybody and to do as Moses had once said, *"Give the Almighty his due, man. Go tell the preachers that you're clean and then lay an offering on the church."*

But the brother was so excited that he was clean again, he went out and told anybody who would listen. Once the info went out on the wire, everybody and his momma wanted Jesus to heal them.

Jesus On The Line

A few day later when Jesus returned to Capernaum, folks got together to come and see Him. Soon there wasn't room for anybody, including Jesus. But He rapped to them anyway.

Anyway, a few minutes into His rap, a group of brothers brought a brother in who couldn't walk. But it was so crowded that they couldn't get through the door. Finally, however, they managed to break through and put the brother down in front of Jesus. *"Brother,"* Jesus told him. *"Your sins are forgiven you."*

The preachers didn't like what they heard. Who was this Jesus who felt He could forgive sins just like that. "No way, man," the scribes said. "You can't do that!"

Then Jesus turned to these wanna-be brothers and said, *"Why do you sit there talking among yourselves, trying to figure Me out? Why don't you just say what you have to say? It don't matter, really, 'cuz you think it would be easier to say, 'Your sins are forgiven' or 'Get up, man, and walk!' Which is it?"*

"Look, here's the deal so you know that the Son of brothers has the power on earth to forgive."

And they didn't know what to say after that, so Jesus turned to the brother and said, *"Get up and walk, my brother. Go on home."* And right away that's exactly what the brother did. He was no longer paralyzed. The brother could walk. And everybody stood 'round with their mouths hanging open. They said, "We've never seen a brother do a thing like this before."

He taught plenty and later He saw a man named Levi sitting down at the tax office. Jesus told him, *"Follow me."* And the brother did. Later they sat around at Levi's house eating with other tax collectors and sinners. Those Pharisees and scribes wanted to know how come Jesus was sitting with them and Jesus heard them.

"The well don't go to the doctor, only sick folks. I don't come to call righteous folks, I've come to call sinners."

Later they wanted to know why His boys didn't fast, and He told them they didn't need to 'cuz He was with them. After a while, Jesus and His boys went into the fields and gathered grain and the Pharisee's wanted to know why the boys were working on a Sunday. Jesus turned to them and said, *"Didn't David when he and his boys were hungry? Didn't they go into the church and eat the bread of the high priests? Didn't you know that? Well, here's the deal. Sunday was made for man, not man for Sunday. So, the son of a brother is also Lord over Sunday. Got it?"*[32]

A Brother's Gotta Do What A Brother's Gotta Do

When Jesus went into the church again, he saw a brother there whose hand was all shriveled up. And those Pharisee brothers were watching to see if Jesus would heal the brother on the day of worship.

So Jesus told the brother, *"Come here, brother man."* And turning to them, He said, *"Tell me. Does the law say you can do good or do evil, to save a brother's life or let him die?"* Those wanna-be brothers had nothing to say, so Jesus had the man stretch out his hand and healed him. But the Pharisees were highly upset and went out and plotted to waste Him.

---

[32]See Matthew, Chapter 12. Also read about the laws regarding the Sabbath or the day of worship in Leviticus, Chapter 24 and Deuteronomy, Chapter 5.

Jesus left and went with his boys out to the sea, but brothers followed Him all the way from Galilee, as far as Judea, Jerusalem and Idumea and even from way past the River Jordan as far as Tyre and Sidon. They wanted to be healed. They wanted to just touch Him as they cried, "We know you're the Almighty's boy." But He warned them not to tell anybody about Him.

Twelve brothers followed Jesus. He chose them 'cuz they would be able to help Him preach and heal the sick. The name of the twelve were Simon, who Jesus called Peter. There was James and John, brothers and the sons of Zebedee. Jesus called them "Men of Thunder." He also chose Andrew, Philip, Bartholomew, Matthew, Thomas, another brother named James who was the son of Alphaeus, Thaddaeus, Simon who was from Canaanite and Judas Iscariot (who would later betray Jesus to the Pharisees).

And Jesus healed many, but those wanna-be brothers, the Pharisees wanted folks to quit seeing Him. "He ain't nobody but the devil," they told the crowd. But Jesus asked them, *"How can Satan drive out Satan? How can a house divided stand?"*[33] He went on to explain the facts of His life to them because they said Jesus had a devil in Him. *"Look, everything will be forgiven the brothers, no matter how much dissing they do, but to diss the Holy Spirit a brother's gonna reap the ultimate payback. He's never gonna be forgiven and that means hell forever."*

---

[33]See Matthew, Chapter 12, verse 25 through 28 and Mark, Chapter 3, verses 23 through 27.

Later, Jesus' momma and His brothers were out looking for Him and when Jesus was told, He said, *"Who is My mother and who is My brother?"* Everybody looked 'round 'cuz they didn't have an answer, so Jesus told them, *"Whoever does what the Almighty wants is My mother, brother, and sister."*

Ain't Nothing But A Word

Jesus taught the folks by telling them stories.[34] He told them the story about the brother who planted and how some of the seeds fell on hard ground, how the birds ate others and how there were those that were planted in some right-on dirt. And then He told them why He told stories 'cuz He said, *"Them that's got shall get, and them that's not shall lose. That's why I tell it this way. For those that are going to be a part of the Almighty's kingdom, these stories are simple. The others just won't get it."* Then He went on to explain what it all meant.

"The seeds are the words of the Almighty. Sometimes that ole devil comes and takes the word from the hearts of the brothers. Sometimes the brothers seem to hear the Almighty, but give it up as soon as they hit bad times. Some brothers hear the word but care only for partyin' and havin' fun.

"But there are some brothers who hear the word and know what to do with it. They are the right-on brothers who get rewarded by the Almighty, Hisself."

---

[34]The stories Jesus told are called parables.

He went on to explain other parables too.[35]

Then Jesus asked the brothers to go with Him over to the other side of the river. When they had gotten halfway across a storm came up and threw the boat here and there. The brothers started begging Jesus to do something. He looked at 'em kind of sad and then said out loud, *"Peace, be still."* He then told the brothers that they were being silly and wanted to know why they didn't have any faith. The brothers didn't say nothing 'cuz they were scared, but they wondered to themselves, "Who is this brother that can make the winds and the waves behave?"

The Healing Power

Now Jesus healed many. He met a brother named Legion who was possessed by a whole lotta demons. He made those demons go into a bunch a pigs. Then He made the pigs jump off the mountain into the sea and drown.

The brother was now OK, but the dudes who saw Jesus' power got real scared and begged Him to get outta town.

He then crossed over to the other side of the sea. They met up with a brother named Jairus who begged Jesus to heal his daughter who was sick. It was no problem for Jesus, but as He started up to the brother's house, a sister who had been bleeding for twelve years touched the hem of Jesus' robe ('cuz she said to herself that if she could only touch the hem she'd be made whole). And right away Jesus

---

[35]Matthew spoke of these same parables or stories in Chapter 13.

knew that something had happened 'cuz He felt the power go out of Himself. *"Who touched me?"* He wanted to know. The sister shyly came forward and stood before Him. *"Daughter. Go on now in peace 'cuz your faith has made you on the one again."*

Now, 'bout the time Jesus got to Jairus' house, everybody told him that the little girl had died. But He told them to hush and asked the ruler to believe. The brothers and sisters laughed at Jesus. He then took Peter, James, and John into the house and in a soft whisper told the girl to wake up. And quick as a flash, the little girl got up and everybody sat around in amazement 'cuz they hadn't seen anything like this before.

They Just Don't Get It

When Jesus went to His hometown, there were those who doubted Him just like the Pharisees. "Who is this brother and where does He come up with these things. Ain't He Joseph's kid? You know Him, the carpenter's son."

But Jesus was aware that a brother ain't often accepted in his own country, so He did what He could, healing a few folks, but the great works He couldn't really do, because the people did not have faith.

He then called the disciples to Him and told them He was sending them out in pairs to preach and heal. He warned them He didn't want them taking nothing for themselves, except a staff and their clothes and shoes. (He didn't even want them taking an extra pair of clothes.) Next, He told them how He wanted them to act and what they should do when things came up.[36] And that's what they did. They preached and begged folks to repent. They also healed the sick and cast out devils.

In the meantime, John the Baptist (who had baptized Jesus) had been put in prison and then wasted by King Herod. Now the word had gone out to Herod 'bout Jesus and some folks told him that Jesus was John the Baptist come back from the dead. Others told him that Jesus was Elijah or another one of those prophets. But Herod wasn't buying it. He knew that Jesus had to be John the Baptist 'cuz his conscious was getting the better of him. You see, Herod had John beheaded 'cuz his lover (who was his brother Philip's wife), sort of tricked him into it.[37] (John had told Herod and his lover that they had no business being together.) The long and short of it was, Herod was shaking in his boots. The friends of John knew what he had done. They came and claimed the body and buried John in a tomb.[38]

Later the disciples got together with Jesus to give Him the line on what they had been doing and where they had been. And Jesus told them to come with Him and rest a while ('cuz they had been so busy they didn't have time to even eat.) They took a boat up to a deserted place so they could rest, but the folks saw them going and many ran on foot to try and catch up with them.

---

[36]See Matthew, Chapter 10. Also, reach Mark, Chapter 6, verses 7 through 11.
[37]See Matthew, Chapter 14. Also see, Mark, Chapter 6, versus 14 through 29.
[38]The equivalent of a graveyard.

When the disciples saw what was happening, they begged Jesus to send them away. "Look, it's late and all. Tell 'em to go away and get something to eat and come back tomorrow."

But Jesus would have none of that. *"We'll give them something to eat."* The disciples then wanted to know how they were gónna feed them. "You want us to go and buy that much bread? With what?"

Jesus asked them how much food they had and they told Him they had five loaves of bread and two fish. So, Jesus told them to have folks sit down. He blessed the food and then divided it up among the twelve brothers. Before it was all over with, everybody had eaten. And not only that, they had 'bout twelve baskets full of food left. All in all, they fed close to five thousand folks.

After a while, He told the brothers He wanted to go up into the mountains to pray. He sent the others away to the other side to Bethsaida. That evening after He prayed, He looked out and saw the brothers rowing hard against the wind while they tried to get to the other side. He walked out to them and would have passed 'em by, except they cried out 'cuz they thought they saw a ghost. But Jesus told them it was He and not to be afraid. Then He got into the boat with them and the wind stopped cold. The brothers were amazed.

Even with all the miracles Jesus performed, including feeding the thousands of folks, some brothers still didn't get it. Yet everywhere they went, folks recognized Jesus and ran to Him. They knew that even if they touched His clothes they'd be all right. Because of how they believed, many were healed and made on the one!

Saying It Don't Make It So

Those Pharisee wanna-be's and some of the other teachers and historians were always trying to jock Jesus. They followed Him 'round like bloodhounds trying to get something on Him. They even had the main line on whether the brothers who followed Jesus washed their hands. There were ways of doing things and these brothers and their Jesus seemed not to care. And those hardheaded folks wanted to know why.

"Why you don't wash your hands like we've all been taught to do?" the Pharisees asked.

And Jesus told them, *"You think what you say makes it so. I don't hold to no traditions that take away from the Almighty. Even Isaiah knew you talked outta both sides of your mouth when he told you what the Almighty said. 'Yeah, they say they honor Me, but it ain't in their hearts. They teach about what brothers say and not what I say.'*[39] *You guys try and figure out ways to do what you want instead of what the Almighty says and I ain't buying it. You even figured a way not to obey the commandments. You know, like, honor your mother and father. So here's how I answer your silly tradition of eating without washing our hands.*

"It ain't what goes in a man that makes him evil 'cuz that goes in, gets digested in his stomach, and passes out.

----

[39]See Matthew, Chapter 23. Also, see Isaiah, Chapter 29, verse 13.

But what a brother says comes from his heart and we all know that evil thoughts can be said. That, my brothers, is the real crime."

After Jesus got near to the towns of Tyre and Sidon, He went to stay at a house in secret. But it wasn't a secret for long 'cuz a woman whose daughter had a devil in her came and begged Jesus to heal the girl. The woman was from outta town and not often accepted, but she begged Jesus anyway 'cuz she knew He had the power. And Jesus told her it wasn't good to give good food to the dogs, but she told Him that even dogs got crumbs, to which Jesus told her she had more faith than most and healed her daughter with a word. The woman went home and found her daughter alive and well.

Leaving Tyre and Sidon, they brought to Him a brother who couldn't hear and talked funny. Jesus said, *"Open up."* And quick, like a rabbit, the brother could hear and speak real clear. Jesus told the brother not to tell anybody, but just like everybody else, the brother couldn't keep his mouth shut. He just had to tell.

Whole Lotta Shaking Going On

Everywhere Jesus went, thousands of folks were waiting to hear Him, to touch Him, and to see Him. Jesus had feelings for them 'cuz many waited without sleep or food, so He told his boys, *"Look, these folks have followed Me for three days. To send 'em away would be stupid 'cuz most of them wouldn't make it. Let's feed them."*

"With what?" the brothers wanted to know. They only had seven loaves of bread and they were way out in the desert with no stores around. Again, just like before, Jesus blessed the seven loaves they had and fed them. This time there was close to four thousand people.

Afterwards, Jesus went with His boys to the town of Dalmanutha. Right away, the Pharisees wanted to test Jesus. They asked Him for a sign. But Jesus told them that no sign was to be given to them.

Later, when they were all in the boat going to the other side, Jesus found out that the disciples had forgotten to take bread so that they only had one loaf. Jesus looked at the brothers and said, *"Don't be hardheaded like the Pharisees or that pigheaded Herod."*

And they thought he was mad at them 'cuz they forgot the bread, but Jesus was hipped to what they were thinking. *"What's with you guys? This ain't about bread. Are you so stubborn that you can't hear or see what is going on?"* Then He asked them, *"How many baskets of leftover bread did you take up when we fed five thousand?"*

They answered, "Twelve."

"And how many this time?"

And they answered, "Seven."

"So how come you don't understand?" Jesus asked.

In Bethsaida they brought to Jesus a brother who was blind. And Jesus put His spit on the brother's eyes and asked him what he saw. The brother answered, "I see brothers like trees, walking."

Again Jesus put His hands over the brothers eyes and then asked him what he saw. The brother answered that he saw everybody real clear. Jesus told the brother not to go into town and tell anybody, but that was like talking to a brick wall.

Next, Jesus and His boys were near the towns of Caesarea Philippi and He asked them, *"Who are the brothers saying I am?"* So, they told Him that some folks thought He was John the Baptist, while others said that Jesus was Elijah or one of those other prophets.

He asked Peter, and Peter said, "You're the Christ, man." Jesus asked them not to tell anyone, though.

After a while, Jesus told the disciples that they needed to know what was about to go down. He told them that He was gonna be wasted by those wanna-be brothers. But Peter would have none of that. He said that he would not allow such a thing to happen, but Jesus told him off. Jesus told him that he didn't know what he was talking about 'cuz he was talking like a brother and not as one of the Almighty's chosen.

When He talked with the folks, He told them that, *"If you want to follow Me, you gotta put yourself last, take on this burden or cross and follow Me. 'Cuz what good is it if a brother has everything in the world, but loses his own soul? You tell me, what will a brother give for his soul? If you're ashamed of Me and My words in front of these adulterous and sinful brothers, you can look for the same in front of My Father, the Almighty."*

So, You Wanna Be First

Jesus told the disciples that there would be some people who would not die before they saw the Almighty's kingdom. He then took Peter, James, and John high up on the mountain a few days later and there He seemed to simply glow.[40]   And up there on the mountain appeared Elijah and Moses, alongside Jesus, so that Peter whispered to Jesus afterwards, "Let us make three churches up here; one for You, one for Moses, and one for Elijah."   The brothers were really afraid and no one knew what else to say.   Soon they heard a voice that said out loud, *"This is My Son and He pleases Me greatly."* Suddenly the brothers saw that only Jesus was with 'em. He made 'em promise not to tell what they'd seen until He'd risen from the dead.

So the brothers didn't tell no one what they'd seen, even they couldn't figure out what He meant by risin' from the dead.

When Jesus and the brothers came down from the mountain, a large crowd of people ran up to Him.   Jesus asked the scribes, *"What's up with the crowd?"*

Then a man out of the crowd answered, "I'm bringing You my son 'cuz he's got some kind of spirit that throws him around and makes him foam at the mouth. I asked Your boys to help me, but they couldn't."

Jesus was upset. He didn't know how long He'd have to deal with these brothers with no faith, but He had the brother bring His son and cured him of the bad spirit. Later when the disciples asked why they couldn't cast out the demons, Jesus told them, *"That kind of demon only comes out by praying."*

Later, Jesus reminded the brothers that someone would betray Him. When they arrived in Capernaum, He asked

---

[40]The Bible says that Jesus was *transfigured.* See Mark, Chapter 9, verse 2.

them why they were arguing about who would be first. This shocked the brothers 'cuz it was true. They had been fussing about who would be first.

"You don't get it. Anyone who wants to be first gotta be last and serve everybody else first." Then He brought a little child to him and sat him on His knee. As he placed his arms around the little kid, He told His disciples, *"When you handle a little kid like this, in My name, you can also handle Me. And understand this, if you handle it well, you handle the Almighty's program altogether."*

John ran up to Jesus and told Him that there were others who were casting out demons in His name, but didn't follow like they did.

"Don't you know that if a brother is for us he can't be against us? As sure as My name, any brother who hands you a cup of water in My name will be rewarded. And know this, that anyone who causes another to fall or turn away from Me, it'll be better for a rock to be hung 'round his neck and be thrown into the sea.

"If your foot makes you sin, cut it off. Better to limp into heaven than have two legs in hell. If your eye makes you sin, take it out. Better to see heaven with one eye than be looking at hell forever with two."

Precious In His Sight

When Jesus came to the other side of the Jordan River, the folks still followed Him, so that He taught them to be on the one with the Almighty. Those Pharisee brothers were still lurking about, however, trying to trip Jesus up.

They even asked about marriage 'cuz they knew the law. The problem was, they didn't know the Almighty.

Jesus said, *"The Almighty made the brothers and the sisters. And when they marry the two become one. What the Almighty has joined together man should not break apart."*

People even brought their children to meet Jesus, but His disciples felt that children were a nuisance and so they tried to tell them to get away. Jesus wasn't having it, and he told those brothers just that. *"Let the little children come to Me and do not keep them away. You brothers hafta be like little kids to enter heaven."* Then He blessed the kids.

Jesus ran into this rich young brother who ran things in his country, and the brother asked Him, "My good brother, what can I do to get a piece of the action to eternal life?"

Jesus answered, *"Only the Almighty is good, my brother. But you know the commandments: 'Don't mess 'round with someone else's ol' lady,' 'Don't waste nobody,' 'Don't take what ain't yours,' 'Don't lie,' 'Give honor to your parents.' You know these?"*

And the brother answered Him, "Yes, sir. I've done these things all my life."

"Okay, then. The only thing you need to do is give up all your money to the poor and take up the cross and follow me."

This saddened the brother big time. He didn't know what to say 'cuz he was really rich.

Jesus felt for the brother, but He used this as an example to let folks know that it was easier for a camel to go through the eye of a needle than for rich brothers to get into heaven 'cuz they didn't know how to let go of the material world.

Peter started to say, "We've done that and followed You." But Jesus answered him before he was even finished. "Yeah, I'm saying you ain't seen nothing yet for those who have given up everything for Me and the gospel. It'll come back to you a hundred fold, including eternal life."

Then Jesus told them that a plot was brewing and it wouldn't be long before He'd be wasted. But they weren't to worry, 'cuz on the third day He would rise again.[41]

Later the sons of Zebedee, James and John asked Jesus if they could sit on His right and left when things got righteous, but Jesus was firm with them. *"You don't even know what you're asking for. You think this thing you want is without sacrifice? And anyway, it ain't mine to give to you. Only the Almighty in heaven can."*[42]

And the others were jealous that James and John even asked, but Jesus told them they were all just like those Gentile brothers who think they're hot stuff when they're not. *"You gotta understand that being hot stuff means being a servant to everybody. And I mean everybody, including Me. The Son of Man came to give His life to save many brothers."*

---

[41]See Matthew, Chapter 20, verses 17 through 19. Also see Mark, Chapter 10, verses 32 through 34.
[42]See Matthew, Chapter 20, where the boys' mother asked Jesus to have her sons sit on his left and right. Also, see Mark, Chapter 10, verses 35 through 45.

On the road to Jericho, they ran into a large group of folks, but on the side of the road sat a blind beggar named Bartimaeus who begged Jesus to have mercy on him. Folks tried to shush him 'cuz he was making a racket, but Jesus wasn't having it and called the brother to Him. And because the brother had faith that Jesus could do the deed, in a flash he could see again.

King of the Road

Soon Jesus came to Jerusalem and He sent His two boys into town to get a colt, telling them that if anybody tried to stop them they were to say that the Lord has need of it. They'll hand it over. And it was just like Jesus said, so they brought the young colt to Him. They spread their clothes on the colt for Jesus to ride and the people of the town spread out branches and clothes, hollering, "Hosanna! Blessed is He who comes in the name of the Almighty." And they also blessed ol' King David while Jesus went into the church.[43]

The next day, Jesus saw a fig tree and 'cuz He was hungry decided to get some figs. But no figs grew on the tree, so Jesus told the tree that it would never grow fruit again. And the brothers heard Him say it.

At the church in Jerusalem, Jesus had to drive off those woeful brothers who used the church to sell their things instead of using the church as a house of prayer.

And this made the Pharisees and scribes real mad, and they plotted harder to find a way to waste Jesus real

---

[43]See Psalm 118, verses 25 and 26.

soon.[44] They didn't like that the people were beginning to believe what Jesus was laying down.

In the morning, the brothers saw that the fig tree had shriveled up and died, so they asked Jesus what was up. And Jesus taught them what faith in the Almighty really meant. *"You can say to the mountain, 'jump into the sea,' and it'll happen. So, I say to you if you pray and also believe, it's gonna happen. And if you ain't on the one with somebody, forgive 'em so the Almighty can continue to forgive you."*

Soon they ran back into those head honchos who tried laying a trap for Jesus. "Tell me, preacher boy, what gives you the right to do the things you do?"

Jesus looked them square in the eye, *"I tell you what. You tell Me something then I'll answer you. The baptism of John, was it from heaven or the brothers? Whata you say?"*

And this scared them 'cuz if they answered "from the brothers," they thought the folks in town would get mad 'cuz everybody thought John a prophet, and if they said "from heaven," they'd wanna know why they didn't believe him when he preached, so they said, "We don't know."

"Then I ain't telling you either," Jesus said and walked off.

---

[44]See Matthew, Chapter 21, verses 12 through 16. Also see Mark, Chapter 11, verses 15 through 19. In Isaiah, Chapter 56, verse 7 and Jeremiah, Chapter 7, verse 11, these prophets told that Jesus would clean out the "den of thieves."

They Still Don't Get It

Jesus told the brothers stories so they would know what's what. He told of a brother who rented out his vineyard. He was supposed to get some of the fruit as rent. But when he sent his boys to collect, they were beaten or killed. Finally he sent his own son to take care of it, but those bad dudes wasted him too.

"*So,*" Jesus asked the brothers. "*What would the owner do now? He'd knock some sense into their heads and give the land to someone else.*"

Then those wanna-be brothers, still tryin' to get Him in trouble with the law, asked Him if it was OK to pay taxes.

Jesus asked for a coin and showed them the king's picture on it. "*Give to Caesar the things that are Caesar's and to the Almighty the things that are His.*"

Even Herod's guys got into the act, trying to trick Jesus into saying something wrong or insulting. They asked Him about the resurrection ('cuz they didn't believe in it anyway), but Jesus was hipped to everything they were trying to do.[45] He had to tell them that the Almighty was the God for the living not the dead.

The teachers of church law were no better. They were trying to trip up Jesus. They asked Him about the greatest commandment of all and when Jesus answered them, "*To love the Almighty, above everything else, with your whole heart and soul and more than that, the second commandment is to love one another just like you love yourself.*"

---

[45]See Mark, Chapter 12, verses 18 through 27.

And the brothers had to agree with Jesus, saying, "Yeah, you're right. To love one another is greater than any burnt offering you could offer."

Jesus told them they were on the one and close to the Almighty's kingdom with that. No one dared to ask another question.

While teaching, Jesus asked, *"How can you say that Christ is the son of David when David, himself, called Christ the Lord? Tell me."*[46]

Jesus warned the disciples and the people He taught that they needed to beware of the ones who dress up, talk fancy, and pretend 'cuz they were simply wolves ready to eat 'em up the first chance they got. Later, He showed them what giving was all about when He watched the rich give a lot, but one poor widow sister gave up all she had, which wasn't much, but in the eyesight of the Almighty it was more than all those rich folks put together.

A Happening On the Mount of Olives

After Jesus left out of the church, one of His disciples wanted Him to look at the great buildings, but Jesus told Him not one brick would stand when it all came down.

Up on the Mount of Olives, Peter, James, John, and Andrew asked Jesus to tell them when everything would go

------

[46]See Mark, Chapter 12, verse 35 through 37. Also see, Psalms, Chapter 110, verse 1, where David says, "The Lord told The Lord, sit down on my right 'til I make your enemies something for you to rest on."

down, and Jesus told them not to be fooled.[47] *"Many folks gonna brag that they're on a first name basis with the Almighty, but it ain't so. I say to you you gotta watch and pray 'cuz you don't wanna be found sleeping on the job. No sir!"*

The Plot Thickens

Now Jesus had warned His boys that they were planning on wasting Him the first chance they got. He knew He had a few days, though 'cuz those cowards didn't want to waste Him during the Passover feasts 'cuz it might make folks mad.

Jesus headed on down to Bethany to Simon the leper's house. There a woman came to Jesus with an expensive bottle of oil and poured it over Jesus' head. This made the disciples angry 'cuz they felt she could have given them the oil to sell for money to feed the poor. Jesus stopped them cold, though, telling them that she was being moved by the Spirit, 'cuz she was simply preparing His body for burial.

Jesus knew what He was talking about 'cuz Judas Iscariot went right to the head honchos and offered Jesus to them for a few pieces of gold. But Jesus knew the score and He prepared to have His last meal with the brothers anyway. He even told them that one of them was gonna turn Him in 'cuz the deed was already done.

---

[47]See Matthew, Chapter 16, verse 18 and Chapter 24, verses 3 through 44. Also, see Mark, Chapter 13, verses 3 through 37.

At supper, He started a new tradition, giving them bread as a sign of His body. *"Take and eat: This is My body."* And He gave them wine saying, *"This is My blood which will be shed for many."* And He told them that when the Almighty's program came down, it would be wonderful for all of them and they would drink new wine in the Kingdom of the Almighty.

After dinner, they went back up to the Mount of Olives where Judas did the deed. But before it happened, Jesus warned them all that they would scatter like the wind, even though Peter tried to deny it. But Jesus knew that He would see them again, so He didn't fuss with them. He just asked them to watch while He prayed. But the brothers couldn't handle even that simple request, so that soon it was the time when Judas would betray them and they weren't prayed up in the least.[48] And sure as shooting, when it all came down the brothers left with nothing but dust behind them.

And, of course, it was all as Jesus had said. Folks lied on Him and said things to get Jesus in trouble, but Jesus had nothing to say.

Outside, it was just like Jesus had said, Peter was watching, but when he was pointed out, he told folks he didn't even know Jesus.

They beat Jesus and mocked Him, telling Him He needed to die. The head ministers then told the folks, that was enough for them. Jesus was arraigned and sent to the Judge, Pilate himself.

----

[48]See the betrayal of Jesus in Matthew, Chapter 26, verses 47 through 56. Also see Mark, Chapter 14, verses 43 through 50.

Here Comes The Judge

Taking Jesus in front of Pilate was simply a formality. Pilate asked Jesus if He was king of the Jews and Jesus told him it was as he said. But to those wanna-be, swoll-headed, church-going, ministers, He said nothing.

"Hey, man," Pilate urged, "If you don't say nothing they're gonna hang you." But still Jesus was quiet which simply amazed Pilate. Pilate had no intentions of doing anything unpopular. Every year during the holidays, he paroled one prisoner. If the people asked for Jesus, he'd give Him to them. If they wanted this brother named Barabbas, a murderer, he'd trade him for Jesus. Either way, as long as he looked good, it didn't matter. The people wanted Barabbas free and Jesus nailed, so that was as it was. But it wasn't done until they had their fun with Jesus and after they finished banging Him around, they took Him out to a place called Golgotha and nailed Him to a cross. They gave him bitter wine and gambled for His clothes and they hung a sign over His head which said, "THE KING OF THE JEWS."

They hung two robbers on either side of Him and waited to see if Jesus would save Himself and made fun when it didn't happen. Later, as Jesus was dying He cried out, *"Eloi, Eloi, lama sabachthani?"*[49] But the folks thought He was calling on Elijah and waited to see, but nothing happened until Jesus breathed His last breath. At that moment, the walls of the church tore clean in half and even one soldier had to say, "Yes. This brother was truly the Son of the Almighty."

---

[49]It means, "My God, My God, why have you left Me."

When it was evening, Joseph of Arimathea, who had money and status, but believed in the coming of the Almighty's kingdom, came and asked Pilate for Jesus' body. After Pilate confirmed that Jesus was dead, he gave up the body so that they could wrap it in fine linen and place it in a tomb. And sitting close by were His friends, Mary Magdalene and Mary, the mother of James and Joseph.

A Day of Rejoicing

Now, Saturday had passed since Jesus died, and Mary Magdalene and Mary, along with Salome, bought spices so that they could anoint his body. They came 'round dawn on Sunday, but stopped 'cuz they wondered who would move that big stone outta the way. Then they looked and saw that the stone had already been rolled away and sitting on the right side of the tomb was a brother dressed in white.

"Don't be afraid," he told them. "I waited here to tell you that Jesus is not here. He wants you ladies to go and tell the others that He is risen! You hear me?"[50]

But the sisters were afraid. They didn't want to tell anybody 'cuz who would believe them? But the first sister to see Him was Mary Magdalene, the same sister Jesus cast out seven demons,[51] and she went and told the others, but they didn't believe.

---

[50]See Matthew, Chapter 28, verse 6. Also see Mark, Chapter 16, verses 6 through 7.
[51]See Luke, Chapter 8, verse 2.

Even after Jesus appeared to a couple of other brothers, and they told the others, they were not believed. It finally took Jesus showing Himself to all of them, so that they could believe and He talked about the brothers bad. How could they not believe when He told him what would happen?

"Go into the world and preach the gospel to everybody. And those that believe will be saved. The signs are simple. If you use My name, you can cast out devils, but you can also speak with new tongues. Even if a brother grabs hold of a deadly serpent or drinks poison, they won't be hurt. All they gotta do is place their hands on the sick and they will be well."

After Jesus had said His piece, He went straight to Heaven to sit at the right hand of the Almighty. And the brothers went out and preached everywhere to everyone, with the Lord's help, making sure of the Word through the signs He talked about. Amen.

The end of the Book of Mark.
May the Almighty bless the reading of His Word!

The Word According to Luke

Luke was a doctor who was also a Gentile. He was one of the people Jesus came to call to the Kingdom of the Almighty. Luke wrote about how Jesus made a difference in the lives of the poor, the Gentiles, and women. Luke also wrote the Book of Acts.

How It All Started

Luke wrote to one of the brothers he ran with, "Although many have taken a stab at writing about Jesus' life, especially those that were there, it seems to me that because I understood what went down, I, too should write an on-the-one account, my friend Theophilus. So here's the info, my brother, so that you will know what is expected of you."

When Herod was King of Judea, there lived a brother who was a preacher named Zacharias. His wife's name was Elizabeth. Both of them lived a decent life for the Almighty, working for Him and keeping His ways. All was well with them except they wanted children and didn't have any.

One day an angel appeared to Zacharias and told him not to be afraid 'cuz he was gonna have a son who was to be called John. "From the beginning," the angel told him, "the boy will be filled with the Spirit and won't drink any of the hard stuff. He'll also be responsible for turning folks back to the Almighty."

And Zacharias wanted to know how this could be since both he and his ol' lady were old.

"Look, man, I'm Gabriel, the angel of the Almighty and He sent me here to tell you these things. But, since you didn't believe me you ain't gonna be able to talk until it all comes down the way the Almighty said it would."

And when Zacharias came out of the church, he couldn't speak. The folks wondered if maybe he had seen a vision. Little did they know. Later, Elizabeth did get pregnant, but she hid herself until she was sure what was going on.

In the meantime, an angel had appeared to a woman named Mary and told her that she was going give birth to the Messiah (the little brother who would be called Jesus).

"Dear Sister, girl, you are truly blessed. You are truly blessed among sisters. Look, don't be scared. The Almighty has a plan."

"That doesn't make much sense. How? I don't know any brother. I mean, not in that way," she said blushingly.

"It gonna be through the work of the Holy Spirit and when it goes down, you'll have a son who will be the Almighty's own."

He also told her about her cousin Elizabeth who was to have a son and what a miracle it was. After Mary conceived, she went to see Elizabeth in the hill country of Judea and immediately upon meeting, the baby in Elizabeth's womb jumped for joy, causing Elizabeth to be filled with the Holy Spirit. And Elizabeth was overjoyed 'cuz she knew then that Mary was truly blessed.

Mary then sang this song:

"My soul says that the Almighty is great!
My spirit rejoices that the Almighty is my savior.
I was just a lowly sister, but He's allowed me to be called blessed. The Almighty is truly mighty.
For He has done great things for me.
From generation to generation He has shown His strength
And He has scattered those proud peacocks to the wind.
He has pulled down the mighty from their thrones
And the rich He sent away with nothing to lend.

He has filled the hungry so that they hunger no more
And remembered his promise to Abraham to send
Someone who would continue his legacy as it was
told
That forever his seed would last until time ends.

Mary stayed with Elizabeth for about three months. Elizabeth had her baby, John, soon after and everybody was real happy for her. When she told folks she was gonna name the baby John, they told her she couldn't do that since no one in her family had been named John. But when they asked Zacharias what he wanted to name the baby, he wrote down the name *John*. Just as he did that, his mouth came open and he was able to speak again.

Zacharias was filled with the Holy Spirit and he told the folks: "Blessed is the Almighty, God of Israel 'cuz He has created a way out for His people. He's always told us that He would save us from our enemies and give us what He promised our fathers. Now it's gonna happen. My son, John, will go out before you preparing a way for The Ultimate Arrival, The Messiah, Hisself. He'll preach that the Almighty is tender and merciful, and that by way of the Messiah the Almighty will give light where there was once darkness."

So, it was that the kid of Elizabeth and Zacharias grew up strong in the spirit. He lived in the desert and cried out for the children of Israel to repent.

Celebration Time

Mary married a brother named Joseph and then had a son named Jesus. Caesar Augustus, the head honcho when

Jesus was a baby, ordered that everybody be registered, so Joseph went to Bethlehem to register Mary and the baby she was to have. Mary went into labor while they were there, so that she had to give birth to Jesus in a manger 'cuz there were no hotel rooms anywhere.[52] And an angel of the Almighty appeared before some shepherds and told them about the baby. Also, in heaven there was a host of angels singing, "Glory to the Almighty and peace to those on earth as well as goodwill toward brothers!" The shepherds, hearing this, went to Bethlehem to see the little boy for themselves and afterwards rejoiced that it was all true. Mary kept things close to her heart and said nothing.

There was a brother named Simeon who was just and honorable. And all he wanted before he died, was to see the Almighty's Son. When Joseph and Mary brought the baby in to be circumcised, Simeon was told by the Holy Spirit that this child was the One! Simeon shouted for joy, then told Mary that while this child would be responsible for the fall and rising of many brothers in Israel, it wouldn't just cause Him pain, it would cause her pain, too.[53]

Anna, a prophetess and daughter of Phanuel from the tribe of Asher, was old and served the Almighty night and day by fasting and praying. Once she lay eyes on the little Jesus, she gave thanks to the Almighty.

When the family went back to Galilee in the city of Nazareth, the boy Jesus grew up and the grace of the Almighty was in Him.

---

[52]See Matthew, Chapter 1, verse 18 through 25.
[53]See Psalm 42, verse 10.

Now according to custom, every year the family went to Jerusalem to celebrate the Feast of the Passover, but when Jesus was twelve, they got almost all the way home before they realized that Jesus was not with them. Turning back, they found Him sitting among the teachers in the church, listening and asking questions. And the wonderful thing was that folks were simply awestruck that this brother was so intelligent. When His parents asked him why He didn't come with them, Jesus told them, *"Don't you know that it is time I'm about My Father's program?"*

But they didn't understand. Mary watched Him grow wiser and stronger in the Almighty's ways, but she said nothing 'cuz she was remembering all that had been said to her.

The Way And The Light

Tiberius Caesar had been head honcho for about fifteen years, Pontius Pilate was governor of Judea, and Herod ran things down in Galilee. John, the son of Zacharias, went 'round telling folks to repent. The prophet Isaiah's words were coming true.

"There'll be a voice hollering out in the wilderness telling ya'll that you better get ready 'cuz the Almighty is on His way with a plan. Get your act together."

John preached about the Almighty's program. When one of those wanna-be brothers came 'round with their nose in the air, he challenged them.

"You guys don't know nothing."

When the tax collectors came to be baptized and asked what they should do to get straight, John told them to be straight with folks when they picked up their tax bill.

Even the soldiers asked what they could do, and he told them to not jock brothers unfairly.

Each time he baptized someone, he told them that this was only a beginning 'cuz someone tough was coming down the pike. He told them about Jesus and that Jesus would baptize them with something so powerful, it would make what he did nothing short of peanuts.

He even stepped on ol' Herod's toes by telling Herod he had no business sleeping with his brother's wife. Eventually, this kind of talk landed John in jail, but not before he had a chance to baptize Jesus with water.

Afterwards a voice from above said He was pleased with Jesus and a dove came down and sat on His shoulders. Jesus' kinfolks went all the way back to Adam, according to the Almighty's purpose.[54]

When Jesus had been baptized, he was led by the Holy Spirit into the desert where he fasted for forty days while being tempted by ol' Satan hisself!

Putting The Devil On The Run

The Spirit led Jesus up from the little Jordan river and further up in the wilderness to go one-on-one with Satan. And for forty day and nights, Jesus didn't eat anything, so that he was hungry.

And that bad ol' devil came to tempt Jesus into doin' something wrong.

"Hey, brother man. If you are *really* the Almighty's kid, say the word and tell these stones to become bread."

---

[54]For a look at the genealogy of Jesus, see Luke, Chapter 3, verses 23 through 38.

And Jesus answered him. *"It is written that a brother can't live by bread alone. It takes every word the Almighty lays down."*

That devil was clever. He grabbed Jesus and took Him up to the top of a building and made Him look down.

"Come on. Make like Superman and fly. 'Cuz it says in that Word you talkin' about that the Almighty got angels who will take care of You and in their hands they'll be strong enough to carry You so that You won't get crushed on the stones. It says that, don't it?"

And again Jesus told that ol' devil, *"I'll tell you what is written. It says 'don't tempt the Almighty, your Master.'"*

That ol' devil snarled and snorted, but he didn't give up. "Okay, you're so cool. Have a look at this." And he took Him high up on a mountain and showed Him the wonders of the world. Big, golden cities lay before Him.

"You can have all this, my brother, if you just fall down and give me my due," he said slyly. "Think about it."

And once and for all, Jesus gave that devil what-for. *"Get behind me, Satan. You ain't nothing and you know it 'cuz it says that a brother should only serve the Almighty and Him alone. Now git!"*

And the devil had no choice. When you gotta go, you gotta go. And as soon as he had left, the Almighty sent the angels to take care of the brother, Jesus, who was really tired and worn out.

On His Job

The moment Jesus stepped out of the wilderness, He started preaching and telling folks the real deal just like the prophet Isaiah had said.[55] He even read from the Book to the people in church and then told them, *"Today the scripture is fulfilled, just so you know."*

But the folks in Nazareth wanted to know who this brother thought He was 'cuz they remembered that He was the son of Joseph. Jesus told them, *"You think I oughtta do like the lesson and heal my own country? Well, I tell you what? A prophet is never accepted in his own country."*[56]

And Jesus made a lot of folks mad that day with what He was saying. "This boy is out of his mind," some said. And they took Him to the edge of town to throw Him off a cliff, but Jesus was tough enough to just walk away.

Jesus started out performing miracles by kicking a demon out of a brother's body and healing Peter's mother-in-law who was sick.[57] He preached to crowds in Galilee, telling them that He was sent to preach to everybody.

The Almighty Wants You!

Jesus started out preaching alone, but it wasn't long before He started picking brothers to help out. He started out with a few fishermen and told them to follow Him. And they did 'cuz they were drawn into it.

He saw two boats near the lake which had just come in after trying to catch some fish. It was the end of the day and the brothers were kind of tired since they hadn't

---

[55]See Isaiah, Chapter 49, verses 8 and 9.
[56]See Luke, Chapter 4, verses 23 through 27.
[57]See Mark, Chapter 1, verses 29 through 31 and Chapter 5, verse 23.

caught anything, but Jesus asked them to go back out on the lake anyway.

"Throw the nets out, boys. We're gonna catch some fish."

Simon, one of the brothers, looked at Jesus and said. "It's your call, brother, but we ain't caught nothing today." He threw the net out and fish filled the nets so tough, it was breaking the ropes.

"Hey, man," Simon called out to his partners. "Help. Can you believe this?" And then he turned and fell on his knees in front of Jesus.

"Hey, Lord. I'm a sinner. You ain't got no business with someone like me," he said with a bowed head. James and John, his partners sat around with their mouths open.

Jesus smiled at Simon and told him, *"Don't sweat it, man. From now on, you'll be catching brothers instead of fish."* Then he told them to drop everything and to *"come with Me."*

Miracles continued, first with Jesus healing a leper 'cuz he believed, healing a paralyzed brother 'cuz he did, too. But there were those who wanted to waste Jesus 'cuz they didn't like the fame He was getting.[58]

Later Jesus corralled a brother named Matthew (a tax collector) into working with Him for the Almighty. And Matthew threw a party for Jesus, so that those wanna-be brothers started grumbling that if Jesus was the Almighty's brother, why did He eat with sinners? Jesus

---

[58]See Matthew, Chapter 15. Also, see Mark, Chapter 2, verses 6 through 12.

replied, *"I didn't come to call the righteous, my brothers. It's sinners, I want."*

From then on it was on.   They questioned everything Jesus did from fasting[59] to gathering food and healing the sick on a holy day.[60] All in all, they just didn't get the message 'cuz they were too stubborn to want to learn. They plotted to waste Jesus as soon as they could.

Jesus called twelve brothers to be His disciples.[61] And He told them that He wanted them to be strong and do what was right and He laid these things on them.

He told them to remember those who are blessed.

"Brothers who are down in the way the feel, they ain't got nothing to worry 'bout 'cuz the Kingdom of Heaven belongs to them. Even those who feel like they've lost, can be on the one again 'cuz there will be arms 'round 'em to make 'em feel better. And you know those brothers who seem weak and on the bottom of the tadpole, the world is theirs. No kidding. And those folks who always do right, got a kind word to say, a good deed or two to do, it's coming back to 'em in spades. If a brother shows kindness and mercy, it's coming back to him more than he can count. Righteousness is given to those whose hearts are pure and good, for in the end they shall see the Almighty. And those that keep the peace, my brothers, shall be called the Almighty's children.   But, those who are dissed and

---

[59]Read the story in Matthew and Mark, but also Luke, Chapter 5, verses 33 through 39.
[60]See Luke, Chapter 6, verses 1 through 11.
[61]For a list of the brothers, see Matthew, Chapter 10, verses 1 through 8.

stepped on 'cuz they are trying to do the right thing, the kingdom of heaven is theirs.

He warned them about getting caught in the glitter and fame. *"My brothers, if you get caught up with all that, you might as well hang it up. You think you're full now, but you'll know hunger pangs like nothing you've ever felt. And just 'cuz everybody is praising your name, it means nothing if you don't have the Almighty with you. Folks talked good about preachers and prophets before and when they fell, they hit the ground hard."*

Then He told them that loving your enemies was better than loving your best friend.[62] He asked them not to judge one another and that if they are truly on the one with the Almighty, then it'll show up by what they produce. Then He told them not to go 'round calling Him Lord if they didn't mean to do what He said, 'cuz that would make Him hotter than anything. He made sure they understood they were to build on a firm foundation and not sinking sand.

The Jesus Chronicles

Jesus performed miracles left and right. Even the head soldier in Capernaum sought Jesus out, asking Him to heal his servant. And when Jesus was headed to his house, the soldier told Him that He didn't need to come. All He had to do was say the word and he knew his servant would be healed. Jesus was moved 'cuz He hadn't heard faith like that, even in Israel where they knew what the Almighty could do.

---

[62]See Matthew, Chapter 5, verses 39 through 45. Also, see Luke, Chapter 6, verses 27 through 36.

A widow woman of Nain was getting ready to bury her son, when Jesus came into town, and He felt compassion for the woman since this was her only son.

"Don't cry," He told her as He walked over to the coffin of the dead boy. When He got to the boy, He told him, *"Young brother, I say rise."* The little brother rose up and talked with his mother who was awed by what had happened. And everybody was talking 'bout Jesus and what He could do.

A few brothers who ran with John the Baptist came to Jesus. "John wants to know if you're the One or should we look for another?" So Jesus healed the sick and preached to them, and after a while, turned to the brothers and told them, *"Tell John all that you have seen. Let him know that he is blessed who ain't afraid to say he's with Me."*

After the brothers had left He turned to the crowd. *"What did you expect when you went to see John? To see some flimsy reed shaking in the wind? Tell Me, what'd you see? A prophet? Yes, he is a prophet, but he is more, just like Isaiah said: 'Of all the prophets born of sisters, this brother is the greatest of 'em all.'"*[63]

And those that had been baptized by John, believed, but those Pharisees didn't buy it.

"Ya'll ain't never satisfied. John didn't eat bread or drink the hard stuff or wine, yet you said he had a devil. The Son of Man comes eating and drinking, being a friend to the tax collectors and sinners, and you put Me down, too."

One of the Pharisees invited Jesus to grab something to eat at his house and when they got there a sister who

---

[63]See Isaiah, Chapter 40, verse 3.

everybody knew to be a sinner, came over to the house and brought some oil. She had heard that Jesus was visiting and she had to do more than sneak a peek. Well, after she got there she sat at His feet, crying and washing His feet with her tears. She used her hair to dry them. But the Pharisee brother was miffed 'cuz he said to himself, "If He is so hot a prophet, He should know this sister ain't nobody He should be messing with."

"Simon," Jesus said. "Let me tell you a story, my brother. There was a creditor who had two loans out. One brother owed more than five hundred bucks and the other brother owed fifty. Neither had the dough to lay on the creditor, so the creditor went ahead and forgave them." He looked Simon in the eye.

"Now, my man, Simon. Tell me. Which of these two brothers will love the creditor more?"

Simon looked around and finally said, "I, uh, guess the brother who owed the most."

"Absolutely, positively right, my friend. Look, man. This sister did what you should have been doing. She washed My feet, kissed Me and put oil on Me. You just stand there doing what? Nothing!"

Jesus turned to the sister and smiled. "My dear sister, your sins are forgiven 'cuz your faith has saved you."

And from that day forward, sisters from all over were good to Jesus. There was Mary called Magdalene, who Jesus had to cast out seven devils, Joanna, who was Chuza's ol' lady (Chuza worked for Herod) and Susanna. But that was only a few of the sisters who graced Jesus presence.

Story Time

Jesus used stories to help folks understand the real deal about the Almighty and His program. There was the story about the brother who tried to grow some seeds. The brother threw some seed on the ground and the birds ate it up. Some of the seed fell on rock, some in thorns, and the plants couldn't grow. But some of the seed ended up in good ground and grew until it gave the most and the best fruit.

Then He would explain the story to His disciples saying, *"I want you to know the secrets 'cuz everybody that hears ain't gonna understand."* He told them that the seed is the word of the Almighty and that there are many ways the word doesn't get through. When the word gets heard it is really awesome.[64]

He told about the lamps and light 'cuz He wanted them to understand that things done in the dark gotta come to the light.[65]

One day Jesus' mother and brothers tried to see Him, but couldn't reach Him through the crowd. When He was told they were there, He answered, *"My family are all those who hear the Almighty's words and do what He says."*

Another day He and the brothers got in a boat to cross a lake. Jesus lay down to nap. Meanwhile a storm came up and the boat was filling with water and about to sink.

---

[64]See Matthew, Chapter 13. Also, see Mark, Chapter 4.
[65]See Matthew, Chapter 5, verses 14 through 16. Also, see Mark, Chapter 4, verses 21 and 22.

Those scaredy-cat brothers woke Jesus. "We're gonna die!"

Jesus got up and told the wind and waves to stop. And everything got real calm.

He turned to the brothers. *"Where is your faith?"* And they were afraid, wondering who could command the winds and water.

In the country of Godarenes, He healed a brother with unclean spirits called Legion; gave a little girl back her life; and healed a sister who had been bleeding for twelve years after the doctors had given up.[66]

After He taught the twelve brothers He called disciples, He tested the waters by sending them out to preach, heal the sick, and pray out devils. And He showed them the kind of miracles that were truly on the one. No one could touch Him, 'cuz what He laid down was real tough.

It was also around this time that John the Baptist was slaughtered 'cuz Herod was weak for this woman. They chopped off John's head because Herod's woman was one bad lady. She didn't want John messing up her good thing.

One day when Jesus and His boys had worked exceptionally hard and folks just wouldn't quit, Jesus decided to feed everybody. This was too much for the brothers to understand 'cuz they didn't have much food and no way to get any more and there were five thousand men, women and children to feed.

Jesus understood though, and told them, *"Make them sit in groups of fifty and there'll be plenty to eat."* Then He

---

[66]See Matthew, Chapters 8 and 9. Also, see Mark, Chapters 5 and 6.

took up five loaves of bread and two fish, prayed to the Almighty and fed every single brother and sister that was there.

Later, when they were all back from their different journeys He asked them if they knew who He was.

A couple of the brothers said they heard Jesus was Elijah, back from the dead. The others agreed, or said that He was one of those prophets. But when Peter was asked, Peter said, "You're the Christ, man. Ain't no doubt."

Jesus explained to the brothers what He was going to have to go through and what would happen to each of them. He told 'em that He would suffer many things, that He would be rejected by the preachers and the lawyers, and that He would be killed. He added that He would rise on the third day.

And He went up on a mountain to pray and a glow came upon Him that was smoother than smooth.[67] And the brothers thought they saw Jesus standing there with Elijah and Moses, and were scared out of their wits. They even heard a voice say, *This is My Son, that I love. Hear Him.*

Later, Jesus healed a young boy who had demons, and He told those demons to get out! And they did.[68]

Who's On First?

Jesus told the brothers again that somebody was plotting His demise, but they didn't want to hear it 'cuz it

[67]The Scripture says He was transfigured and His garments were white as snow. See Matthew, Chapter 16, verse 28.
[68]See Mark, Chapter 9, verses 14 through 17.

scared them. But they did argue among themselves about who was the greatest. Jesus handled it this way. He put a little kid on His lap and told them that anybody who wanted to be the most, they better first learn to be the least. He told them, *"More than that, if you welcome even a little kid like this one, you just received Me and you know that means you've received the Almighty."*

So they got on another kick. John wanted Jesus to stop those brothers who tried to copy their act, but Jesus told them that anyone for us ain't against us, and told John to sit on it.

When they came to the town where the Samaritans lived, the disciples wanted to show how tough they were just 'cuz the Samaritans didn't want 'em around. "You want us to order some fire to burn these sorry brothers?" James and John asked.

But Jesus just shook his head. *"Ya'll don't even understand what you ask. I didn't come here to waste anybody. I came to save."*

Jesus tried to get them to understand, but they didn't always. One of the boys said, "Jesus, I'll follow you anywhere. You know that."

And Jesus answered, *"Everybody got a place, but Me. Even foxes have holes and birds nests, but I ain't even got a place to lay My head."*

Still, another brother wanted some time off to go bury his father, but Jesus told him to let the dead bury the dead. The brother had work to do.

And another asked if he could just go and say good-bye before they left, but Jesus warned the brother that once your hand is on the wheel, you oughta look forward not backwards.

Jesus then called seventy others and sent them out just like the others, two by two, into every city around. He wanted them to know that there were lots of folks who needed their help, but not enough workers to go around. And He warned them about how they were to conduct themselves if they wanted to hold on to their jobs.[69] Those seventy were tough. They went out and did the job like they were supposed to and Jesus said, *"Right on, brothers. I saw it. Satan fell like lightnin' to the ground. You've got the power, I tell you, but don't go gettin' the big head 'cuz you can cast out devils. Just be glad your name is written in the book of the Almighty."*
Jesus was overjoyed 'cuz things were righteous and He knew that it happened 'cuz the Almighty wanted it to happen. Turning to His boys, He told them. *"You can't even begin to know how much you guys are blessed. You'll get to see things the great prophets and mighty kings never saw."*

Jesus was always being tested. Once this lawyer asked what a brother had to do to get eternal life. And Jesus turned it back on him and asked him to say what the law said. After the brother told about love the Almighty and your neighbor as yourself, Jesus told this story.
"There was a brother who went down to Jericho and a bunch of bad dudes beat him up pretty bad. The brother

---

[69]For more on the seventy send by Jesus, read Matthew, Chapter 10.

was half dead. A preacher was coming down that same road and when he saw the brother lying half dead, he didn't want to become involved so he crossed over to the other side. The same thing happened when a Levite brother saw what had gone down. He looked and then crossed over to the other side 'cuz he didn't want to get involved. But a Samaritan brother came to the scene, he looked and saw that the brother needed his help and gave it to him. He went all out, including taking him to a hotel to rest. He laid some cash on the hotel manager, telling him that if any more money was needed it wouldn't be a problem.

"Now, sir, which brother was the neighbor to the fallen brother?"

The lawyer answered, "The brother who helped him."

"Yeah, you're right. Now do the same."

Later, Jesus went to a town and visited a sister named Martha. Martha's sister was Mary and they welcomed Jesus to their home. However, Mary just sat and watched Jesus, hanging on to His every word. Finally, Martha spoke up 'cuz she wanted Jesus' opinion. "Don't you think it wrong that my sister isn't up helping me serve You?"

Jesus answered, *"Come on, Martha, this ain't the only thing bothering you. But your sister has chosen to do a good thing 'cuz it won't be long before I'm taken away from her for a long time."*

Nobody Knows The Trouble I Feel

The brothers wanted Jesus to teach them to pray and Jesus said, *"When you pray, say something like this:*

'Our Father in heaven, Your name is so wonderful. We want Your kingdom right now, but it's gotta be what You want, both here on earth and in heaven. Right now we're asking that You give us that day to day thing that You do so well, nourishing and feeding us, but forgive us for being so sinful. And just like You forgive us, we'll forgive each other 'cuz that's what You said. And one more thing, Lord, we ask that You put a hold on those things that tempt us to diss You and do wrong 'cuz the devil is on the loose. Deliver us from him. Amen!'"

Jesus let them know that friends may come calling at midnight and the door may or may not be opened, but if you pray to the Almighty, keep asking, and it will be given to you; knock and the door will open 'cuz everybody receives from the Almighty. You give to your son, don't you? Well, your Father in heaven is much bigger than you.[70]

But every time He did something wonderful, there was always some wanna-be brother who felt that Jesus was some devil 'cuz He put the devil on the run. But Jesus let them know that it couldn't happen in this life and certainly not by His hand.

"How does a house stand if it's divided? Can you tell Me that? You think Satan's house would stand if folks were trying to cast him out? It would happen. If I'm doing the devil's work, tell Me, who do your sons work for? Let them

---

[70]See Matthew, Chapter 7, verses 7 through 12 and Chapter 21, verse 22. Also, see Mark, Chapter 11, verse 24.

*be the judge. When a brother is taking care of his own, he
can rest in peace 'cuz he'll be on guard and won't let up.
But I'm telling you that if a brother comes along who's a
whole lot tougher and badder, he takes what he wants
from the brother. Everything becomes his. Look, everybody who ain't for Me, is against Me. And them that are
against Me, better look out 'cuz I'll scatter them to the
winds."*

Jesus also let folks know what happens once a spirit
leaves. *"If he can, that mean ol' spirit comes back with
friends, ready to take up residence again."*

Jesus also got back at the brothers 'cuz they were always
saying they wanted some sign, but they didn't see a sign
when it was smacking 'em in the face.[71] Again, He told
them how nobody with a good lamp hides it so no one else
could see.[72]

And still, they tried to trip Him up. Even washing His
hands became an issue for them 'cuz they were so caught
up on the ceremony, they forgot about the Almighty. To
the lawyers, He really jumped all over this attitude 'cuz
they felt Jesus was talking about them. And Jesus let them
know that He was. He told them off in no uncertain
fashion, letting them know that they were not such hot
stuff after all.

He pulled His boys coattails about how they shouldn't
try and act like the Pharisees, but should be
straightforward about everything. He told them not to be

---

[71]See Matthew, Chapter 12, verses 38 through 42. Also, see
Jonah, Chapter 1, verse 17, Chapter 2, verse 10 and
Chapter 3, verses 3 through 10.
[72]See Matthew, Chapter 5, verses 15 and 16. Also, see
Mark, Chapter 4, verse 21.

hypocrites, to fear the Almighty, and to tell folks about Him and not be ashamed. He let them know that they should be on the Almighty's program and not theirs, trying to get rich from the Almighty's work. Mostly, He told them they didn't have to worry 'cuz the Almighty had their back. Their job wasn't gonna be glamorous or without sacrifice, but He wanted them to serve the people and obey the Almighty. He warned them, though, that He was gonna divide the country 'cuz there would be those who followed and those that didn't. But in the end, it was all part of the Big Plan by the Almighty. *"In time,"* He told them, *"You'll understand exactly what's going down and when, and if brothers don't make things right with one another; and pay every last cent owed, it wasn't going to be pretty in the end."*

Sink or Swim

"It don't matter what kind of sin you commit, it's all the same. Unless you say you're sorry and give yourself to the Almighty, it's a one-way ticket to hell.

"It's like this. A brother had a fig tree growing in his yard. Every year he would go up to the tree and there was no fruit. He told his workers to cut it down, but one of the workers offered to fertilize it and help it to make fruit for the next year. And the worker told his boss, 'If it don't grow, then you can cut it down. Deal?'"

One Sunday, Jesus was teaching in one of the churches and a woman who had been bent over for many years was sitting there. Jesus saw her and felt compassion, so He said, *"Sister, straighten up. Everything is on the one."*

And immediately the sister rose and stood straight and tall, glorifying the Almighty. The head of the church was miffed 'cuz he felt Jesus shouldn't be healing anybody on the day of worship. But Jesus called him a hypocrite 'cuz everybody knew that if his ol' donkey was stuck in a ditch, he wouldn't let it stay there until Monday, but would get it out.

Folks asked about what the kingdom of God was like. Jesus answered that it was like a mustard seed. Started small, but it grew and grew.

Over and over, Jesus told stories about what the kingdom of the Almighty was like. He told them to work as hard as they can 'cuz it meant that it was well worth the work. The harder the road, the better the reward.

One brother said to Jesus, "Blessed is the brother who eats bread in the Kingdom of the Almighty."

Jesus told him, *"Yeah, you're right. There was this brother who was gonna give a great supper party and he sent out invitations. One by one, though, all those invited started making excuses. The first brother said, 'Look, I just bought some property and I can't be bothered right now. Sorry.' And the second brother said, 'I just bought some cattle and I gotta get 'em straight. Another time.' And others said no, too. When it got back to the host, he told his employee, 'Go out and get the poor, the injured, the blind. I want any poor soul you can find.' It was done just as he had said and then he told his employees that those so-called 'friends' would never taste his food again."*

But often Jesus was sad, 'cuz he loved Jerusalem, but it was also Jerusalem that killed the prophets when they came to tell the truth. And He let them know how it would all come down 'cuz they hadn't done right by the Almighty.

You Take The High Road and I'll Take The Low Road

Every time Jesus ate with one of those Pharisees, they tried to trick Him, but Jesus always passed the test.

But He also had a line to hang on those wanna-be brothers 'cuz He saw how they wanted to make themselves so important. They thought they deserved to sit at the best table and eat the best food. These brothers also wanted to be seen, but Jesus knew that to truly be hot stuff like they wanted meant they needed to sacrifice and take less, rather than always wanting more, more, more! And He told them another story so they would know what He meant.

"When you go to a wedding, don't sit at the head table. 'cuz someone might say, 'Hey man, give your chair to that other guy.' Then you'd be real embarrassed. Instead sit yourself down at the last table and maybe they'll ask you to sit closer. Then you will be seen as a right-on brother."

And Jesus told yet another story. *"One day a man decided to invite a bunch of his boys to dinner. But everyone he asked had some lame excuse not to come.*

The man had his boys go out into the streets and brought in all the poor, and homeless, and sick. And since there was still room, they asked everyone else they could find. But those sorry brothers who'd made excuses were not welcome."

In order to follow Jesus, one had to give up everything.
Everything and everybody had to come second to the
Almighty and His plan.[73]

Here's Another Story I've Got To Tell

Every story Jesus told meant something to those that
were willing to listen, but those hardheaded Pharisees just
didn't get it. They were so full of themselves, that it just
didn't sink in like it should have.

There was the story of the lost sheep when Jesus told
those folks it was worth going after only one. *"Yeah, it
great that 99 stay. I'm happy, but I dance for joy when the
one who was mine gets lost, then makes it back home. In
fact, there is more joy in the one who asks for forgiveness
than those that never need it."*

There was the story of the lost coin where a woman lost
a coin and spent all day fixing up her house trying to find
it. The sister shouts all day over a lost coin and it happens
the same in heaven. Angels be singing "Hallelujah" over
lost sinners come home.

Of course, there's the story about the sons, one who was
faithful, and the other a hardheaded soul who had to learn
his lesson the hard way.[74] It went something like this:

The youngest boy wanted his inheritance kinda early
since he felt he was all of that. Daddy was cool, giving all
the little brother asked for and the brother took off to the

---

[73]See Luke, Chapter 14, verses 25 through 33.
[74]This story is often called "The Return of the Prodigal
Son" and can be found in Luke, Chapter 15, verses 11
through 32.

big city. Sure enough, the city was too much for him and it wasn't long that Brother Long Pockets was short on cash and all his so-called friends turned their backs 'cuz he had nothing. Not one brother would offer him a dime.

The brother thought about his Dad and how rich he was. He said to himself, "I'm a fool and don't deserve nothing from my ol' man. I'll just beg him for a job 'cuz I ain't fit to call myself his son." And so he went to his Dad's house to ask for a job.

"Daddy," he said slowly, his head bowed. "I'm so sorry. I ain't fit to tie your shoes, but if you'll be kind enough to just give me the worst job you've got, I'll be grateful."

His Dad was overjoyed. His son had come home. It was more than he could ask for.

"Uh uh. Not my son," he said while at the same time motioning for his employees to bring the best for his son. "Fatten the boy up. Put some decent clothes on him," His father said. And the ol' man rejoiced up a storm 'cuz his son had returned home. "He was a lost brother, but now he's found. Let's party 'cuz my boy has come home."

Everybody was happy 'cuz the little brother had come home. Everybody, that is, 'cept his big brother who felt that things had changed. After he found out what was going down, with a big party and all, he went to his Dad.

"Dad, what's up? You ain't never thrown a party for me like this. I haven't given you a moment's trouble. What gives?"

Daddy was patient. "My son, you were always with me. That's good. But your brother here was all but dead and now he's found. Come on. Be glad."

Through all these stories, Jesus was trying to tell them that everybody was worth trying to save and help. Also, judgment belongs only to the Almighty.

And there was more. Some brothers went all way 'round the corner and back just to cross the street. They always do it the hard way. Sometimes, though, the hard way can be the better way when given over to the Almighty.

One brother was about to be fired from his job, so he went to his boss's debtors and asked how much each owed. And as a favor to them, he told them he could cut them some slack on the bill, which he did. In the long run, the brother made friends and no enemies. And oddly enough the boss thought the brother was a shrewd dude.

Jesus told the brothers that if a brother is unjust in a few things he'll be unjust with much. Same goes for the good, too. If you can't handle a little, who is gonna trust you with anything. And He then told them that nobody can serve good and evil, or two masters. Either way it goes, no matter what a brother says, he'll love one and hate the other.

These stories were told to the Pharisees 'cuz Jesus knew how much these brothers loved the cash. It was usually cash over anything for the Almighty and they even tried to justify what they did. They didn't understand that what was so high and mighty to folks on earth was usually nothing to the Almighty.

Then Jesus told another story 'bout the brother who so rich he wore the finest rags in town, made of linen and colored purple, a really fine color to wear. And then there was this begging brother named Lazarus who was so down and out, his body was full of sores and he had to beg for his food. Even the dogs came and licked the sores of the brother 'cuz there was nothing he could do.

Both brothers died, but the poor brother was taken to heaven and the rich dude was sent to hell where it was too hot for words, literally. And the brother in hell could see ole Abraham up in heaven and he begged him to please send Lazarus for a moment just to dip his finger in some cool water and touch his tongue. And the Almighty had to hip the rich cat to the fact that there wasn't anything he could do. Neither could Lazarus, 'cuz there was no bridge from heaven to hell. Abraham tole him that the brother had made his bed in hell and now had to lie in it. But the brother begged for one more favor. He wanted someone to send Lazarus down to rap with his brothers, so they wouldn't make the same mistake.

But Abraham told the brother that if they weren't listening to Moses and all the prophets He sent, they certainly wouldn't care what one poor brother back from the dead had to say.[75]

Don't Mess 'Round

Following the rules was always real important to the Almighty, not so much for Him, but because of the commandments. The Almighty wanted the love of all brothers and sisters, but he wanted them to love one another. Any rule that dissed the Almighty or any brother or sister was real uncool.

---

[75]See Luke, Chapter 16.

Jesus told folks He wanted them to get along, but he was gonna make a brother responsible for hurting another. He considered every brother like His own kid, and hurting His kid was a no-no. If a brother does something to you, you are to forgive him. Even as many as seventy times seven.

And folks wanted to know how they could increase their faith. Jesus told them they didn't need much. *"If you have just a little faith, even as tiny as a mustard seed, you can order a big ol' tree to move itself and it will happen. And it would be better not to go 'round expecting a huge payoff for doing good 'cuz doing good is its own payoff."*

Later Jesus went back toward Jerusalem, and there in a small town, stood ten lepers. They begged Jesus to have mercy on them and He did. The lepers were cleaned up with a word.

Afterwards, one of the brothers came back and thanked Jesus again for healing him. Jesus asked him what happened to the other brothers. Didn't they want to thank the Almighty? He then gave the one lone brother a blessing telling him it was his faith that made him well.

As always, the Pharisees were lurking 'round the corner trying desperately to trip Jesus up. This time they wanted to know when the Almighty was running down His program and bringing His Kingdom. And Jesus told them that their naked eye couldn't tell nothing. *"You won't be able to look up and say, 'There it is' or 'Here it comes,' 'cuz the kingdom of the Almighty is inside you. One day,"* He said to His disciples, *"some folks will try and tell you they know the signs, that they know when and where, but I'm telling you, don't buy it. First things first. Some things are gonna have to go down. I'm gonna have to suffer and not even be accepted before the Kingdom comes. Whether you realize it or not, it'll be just like the days of Noah.*[76] *Folks will be eating and drinking, just like nothing is happening, and bam! There it is. Just like with Noah. No one knew what was happenin' until he shut the door. Just like with Lot;*[77] *in his day it rained fire and brimstone and folks didn't know what hit 'em. Remember Lot's wife? I'm tellin' you, anybody who tries and save his life gonna lose it in the end. It'll go down like this. If there are two brothers sleeping, one will be taken and one left. If two sisters are working side by side, it'll be the same."*

The brothers asked, "Where are they going?"

"To the body of Christ, that's where. There eagles will come together."

Don't Worry 'Cuz the Almighty's Coming

One story Jesus told was about a judge in a certain city who didn't give a hoot about the Almighty or any brother. A sister came to the judge and asked that he help her win a case against her enemy. Well, the judge decided he should help the sister, but not because he was afraid of anybody, just 'cuz he didn't want her worrying him to death. Then Jesus said, *"So, if a brother who ain't with it can help*

---

[76]The story of Noah can be found in Genesis, Chapters 6 and 7.
[77]Lot lived near the towns of Sodom and Gomorrah, which the Almighty destroyed. To read more about Lot, see Genesis, Chapter 19.

someone out, you think the Almighty won't? Why can't
you see that?"

Then He told another story to those brothers who
thought they were so righteous while they talked about
others.

*"Two brothers came to the church to pray. One was a
Pharisee and the other was a tax collector. The Pharisee
brother prayed like this. 'Almighty, I'm so glad I'm such a
cool brother and don't act like those common, sinful
folks—you know, the skirt chasers, thieves, pimps or even
like that tax collector. You know I'm fasting twice a week
now and I give you at least ten percent of my cash. So,
anyway, thanks that I'm so wonderful.' But the brother
who collected taxes, hung his head and wouldn't even look
up at the Almighty. 'Have mercy, Lord, 'cuz I ain't nobody.
I'm just a sinner.' And I'm telling you, the tax collector got
his prayer heard and was lifted up, but the Pharisee was
just another wanna-be in the Almighty's book."*

Folks started bringing their children to Jesus so that He
could just lay even a finger on them, but the disciples
didn't want Jesus bothered with any screaming kids.
Jesus called the children to Him and told His disciples,
*"Don't ever do that again. Let these kids hang out with Me
'cuz anyone who doesn't learn to take this message like a
child ain't going nowhere."*

Jesus even helped a rich young brother understand that
it took more than following rules to get to eternal life. It
took some real sacrifice. It would take the brother giving

up everything. The brother couldn't handle that 'cuz he was real rich.[78]

Because everything was possible with the Almighty, Jesus used the rich brother's problem to drive home a point. It would be easier for a camel to go through the eye of a needle, than any rich dude getting into heaven.[79] Then He warned the brothers that the time was near when the folks would grab Him and take Him to jail, eventually killing Him.

Near Jericho, a blind brother asked Jesus to heal him, so Jesus did. After Jesus passed through Jericho a real short brother named Zacchaeus tried to get to Jesus. Not being able to beat the crowds or see above them, the brother decided that he could climb a sycamore tree to see Him since He was passing that way. Jesus knew the brother was up there in the tree, so He yelled for him to come down. *"Hey, brother man. Come on down 'cuz I wanna stay at your house."*

And folks complained 'cuz they knew the brother to be a sinner and felt Jesus should stay somewhere else. But Zacchaeus wanted to make things right and he told Jesus that not only would he give half of everything he owned to the poor, but anybody he had messed over would be taken care of four times over. And Jesus knew the deal 'cuz He understood. That day He told Zacchaeus, *"Salvation has come to your house, man, 'cuz you are on the one with the Almighty."*

---

[78]See Matthew, Chapter 19, verses 16 through 29. Also, see Mark, Chapter 10, verses 17 through 30.
[79]See Proverbs, Chapter 11, verse 28. Also, see Matthew, Chapter 19, verse 23 and Mark, Chapter 10, verse 23.

Over and over again, Jesus was showing what it took to be on the one with the Almighty. When He got nearer to Jerusalem He told this story 'cuz everybody wanted to see the Kingdom light up the sky right then and there.

"There was this head honcho who went to another country to take a kingdom and then come home. He called ten of his servants to him and handed over some money to each of them. He told the servants to take care of business while he was away. And the folks in town hated the head honcho, but waited until he left to try and throw him over. When he got home after getting the kingdom, he called his servants to come and show what they had done.

"The first came and told him that he was able to make ten times what he had given him. So, the brother made him head honcho over ten cities. The second servant came and told him he was able to make five times what he had been given, so he was made ruler of five cities. But one came and said, 'Look, take your money back 'cuz I didn't want nothing to do with it. I know you're tough and I didn't want you mad with me, so I just kept it. It's yours. I don't want it.' And the head honcho was upset 'cuz he could have at least put the money in the bank and gotten some interest, but he was just too trifling for words. He took the dough and gave it to the brother who had made ten times the amount of money he had been given. And even though the brother already was over ten cities, the head honcho gave him more."

Jesus wanted the folks to know that "them that's got shall get, but them that's not shall lose" 'cuz if you can't handle a little, you sure can't handle a lot.

After Jesus had said all this, He went up into the mountains to pray 'cuz it was only a matter of time before He would be wasted. He sent His disciples into town to get a donkey and horse. And He let them know that taking the animals would be all right. Afterwards, He rode into town on the animals and His disciples were yelling, "Bless the King 'cuz He comes in the name of the Almighty. There'll be peace in heaven and glory to the highest." And the Pharisees wanted Jesus to shush 'em, but He wasn't having it 'cuz if the disciples didn't do it, the rocks would do it for them.

Later Jesus cried 'cuz he knew the folks were both dumb and blind. They didn't know when they had it so good. It wouldn't be long 'fore folks were ground into the dirt by their enemies.

Then Jesus went into the church and saw folks selling their wares when they oughta be worshipping the Almighty. After He sent them packing turning those folks every which way but loose, He spent the rest of the day teaching. And it was while He was teaching that the questions were put to Him about His right to do what He did. He didn't tell them though 'cuz He knew they were only trying to trick Him into saying something to give them a reason to waste Him. It wasn't time. He then taught those who wanted to be taught about the vineyards so that they would know that there was a plot against Him.[80]

"Okay, let me break it down further. There was a certain brother who owned some land where he planted some grapes and then built a wall around it. He also built

---

[80]See Mark, Chapter 12, verse 1 through 12.

a winepress and a tower and rented it to folks who would work the land and bring his grapes in when they were ready. And when it was time to bring in the grapes, he sent folks to bring them to him, but the folks he rented the place to killed one of the brothers and threw rocks at the other. Over and over again, the brother sent folks to try and get his grapes, but they just kept wasting anybody who came. Finally, the brother sent his only son, and you know what? They killed him, too. Now it won't be long before the owner has to come to claim his property. What do you think he'll do to those guys?

"He'll waste those brothers, that's what. Then he'll hire somebody else.

"Don't you guys read? It says in the Word that 'The stone that the builders threw to the side has become the main stone. This was the Almighty's plan all long and ain't it grand.'[81] So here's what I say to you. The Almighty's kingdom will be taken away from you and given to those who will take care of it."

And those big time preachers and politicians got a little antsy thinking that Jesus was talking 'bout them. They didn't like it, so they plotted and planned to waste Jesus at the first opportunity.

They were already trying to trap Him into saying something against the government, but Jesus was too tough for them.[82] Even those backward brothers tried to get in on it and trap Jesus but He was smarter than they could ever hope to be. Since He knew they didn't even believe in the resurrection, their questions were stupid to

---

[81]Read Psalm 118, verses 22 and 23.
[82]See what Jesus had to say about taxes in Matthew, Chapter 22, verse 15 and Mark, Chapter 12, verse 14.

begin with.[83] Of course, the final nail was when they tried to figure out how Jesus could be King David's descendant and Lord. That one threw them.[84]

But lessons were really for the people who came to listen and not judge Jesus like those Pharisees. Jesus saw the rich giving gifts to the Almighty. Then he saw a poor widow putting in her few cents. He told them that her gift was better because it was all she had. The story about the widow showed folks that it wasn't how much you gave, but how you gave.

He also let them know that all that glittered and shined wouldn't last. This knowledge would help them know when the time for the Almighty was right up on 'em. All the stories worked together to let folks know that Jesus was the one and that He knew what He was talking about.[85]

Taking Jesus Out

The plot thickened 'cuz they were closing in on Jesus. It was only a matter of time before they took Him and put on a fake trial on trumped-up charges. It was even shorter after that they would kill Him. First, though, the boys and Jesus had to have one last supper to get their business straight and talk things out.[86]

---

[83]See Matthew, Chapter 22, verses 23 through 33. Also, see Mark, Chapter 12, verse 18 through 27.
[84]See Matthew, Chapter 22, verses 41 through 46. Also, see Mark, Chapter 12, verses 35 through 37.
[85]See Luke, Chapter 21, verses 5 through 38.
[86]See, Matthew, Chapter 26, Mark, Chapter 14 and Luke, Chapter 22.

Jesus took a loaf of bread, thanked the Almighty, and passed it around to the brothers, saying, *"This is My Body, which is given for you. Do this to remember Me."*

Then He took a cup and said, *"This cup holds My promise to you, My Blood, which will be shed for you."*

It was here that Jesus told them that one of them would bring Him down, and it happened just the way He said. The devil made brother Judas turn on Jesus.

After Jesus was arrested, He was beaten and treated cruelly. Then He was handed over to the Governor for sentencing.[87] That was only a formality 'cuz they were planning on killing Him all along. Jesus was hung on a cross and left to die, but it was for the best 'cuz in the end, Jesus cheated death out of its victory. Jesus was on the one as He rose from the dead for the sake of every brother and sister.[88]

After Jesus came back from the dead He took His time visiting with each of the brothers who had followed Him and He told them, *"Don't worry, guys. Look at my hands and feet. It's Me, all right. And I'm for real, 'cuz if I were a ghost I wouldn't have bones and flesh."* And Jesus sat down and ate with them before He had to leave. He promised them a gift greater than anything they had ever received: the forgiveness of sin. He let them know that what had been said in the past had finally come true.

With all that said, Jesus went out into Bethany and He lifted up His arms and blessed them. And before they knew what was happening, He was carried up into heaven.

---

[87]See Matthew, Chapter 27.
[88]See Mark, Chapter 16.

The brothers blessed the Almighty big time 'cuz it was righteous. They cheered until they could no longer see Jesus, and then they cheered some more.

The end of the Book of Luke.
May the Almighty bless the reading of His Word!

The Word According to John

John believed that Jesus was the Son of the Almighty, plain and simple. He should have known, 'cuz he was one of the twelve disciples. John knew who Jesus was and what He could do. He proves it to us by retelling the stories of the signs Jesus performed and what those signs mean to all of us. Things were complete when Jesus came even though some folks didn't believe it was true.

Who's the Man?

From the beginning there was the Word and that Word was with the Almighty, but more than that, that Word *was* the Almighty. Nothing begins or ends without Him, 'cuz He is life and life is the light of brothers everywhere. It shines in the darkness, but the dark doesn't know what hit it.

Now John (the Baptist) was a brother who got to see firsthand about that wonderful Light. That way he could tell folks later 'bout the Light and how it lit his world. He let us know that the Light landed on earth and lived in this world, but we didn't even know it. The Light was so heavy it asked that folks become children of the Almighty even though folks were listening and didn't believe Him. That Light walked this earth like a brother and *was* a brother to all mankind. John saw it and John told it when he said, "He was the Almighty's only son and He was right on time for all of us."

Now folks were always asking if this brother named John the Baptist was the One 'cuz he lived a good life. He told folks he wasn't, so they'd ask him if he was Elijah the prophet. And he said, "Nope. Not me."

"Well, who are you?"

And John said, "I am..." and paused for a moment, "simply a brother crying out in the wilderness asking you guys to get your act together for the Almighty, just like Isaiah said."

"Well, if you ain't *Him* the Christ, and you ain't Elijah, how can you go 'round baptizing folks?"

" 'Cuz I baptize them with water, but there's a Brother right here with us and you don't even know Him. I ain't nobody to even take off His shoes."

And the very next day, who'd John see, but Jesus. John knew exactly who He was as he yelled out, "Here He is, the Lamb of the Almighty. He's gonna take away all the sin of the world. Just like I told you."

The story goes that John baptized Jesus with water and a dove came down and rested on Him 'cuz He was the one who would baptize with the Holy Spirit.[89] This was what John the Baptist said to his boys 'cuz he wanted them to know. Those brothers immediately started following Jesus around until He finally had to ask them what they wanted.

"Rabbi,"[90] they said, "where are you staying?"

One of the brothers was Andrew, brother of Peter. He ran to his brother and told him, "We've found Him. He's the One all right."

Jesus went to a brother named Philip and told him to *"Follow Me."* And he did, but he also told his friend Nathanael the good news, but Nathanael wasn't buying it. He felt nothing but trash came outta Nazareth.

When Jesus saw the brother, He said, *"My goodness. Here comes a brother who'd never lie to a brother."*

Nathanael wanted to know how He knew anything about him. But Jesus told him that He had watched the brother under the fig tree talking to Philip. And

---

[89]See Mark, Chapter 1, verse 10. Also, see Matthew, Chapter 3, verses 6 through 11.
[90]Teacher.

Nathanael knew that the brother had to be the One 'cuz how else could He know that.

And Jesus said, *"You mean you believe me 'cuz of what I said? Well, if that's the case you're gonna have the socks knocked off you 'cuz you ain't seen nothing yet. You're gonna see the angels of the Almighty coming and going on the Son of Brothers."*

Momma Said...

The next day there was a wedding in the little town of Cana, near Galilee. Jesus and his mother were both there hanging out and having a good time at the wedding when the unthinkable happened. The party wasn't even in full swing and they were out of wine.

Mary said to Jesus, "They have nothing to drink."

And Jesus answered her. *"What has this to do with Me. It's not My time yet!"*

But Jesus' mother was already telling folks what to do. "Give Him whatever He asks for," she told them. Jesus told them what He needed and the brothers scampered around trying to get everything together. First they brought in six waterpots made of stone which were cleaned and spruced up real tight. Jesus told them to fill these with water. They poured water all the way to the top. Then Jesus said, "Okay, now take a sip."

That wine was the most wonderful tasting wine ever. In fact, the brother of the feast was impressed big time. He asked the servants, "What gives?"

They shrugged their shoulders even though they knew what Jesus had done was awesome. They just sat there staring. The brother then called to the bridegroom.

"Ain't this the lick?" he told him as he patted him on the back. "Most folks put the good stuff out first 'til folks are so into it they don't know the difference when he puts out the bad stuff. But you," he said with admiration, "saved the best for last."

And this was the first miracle Jesus performed. From there, Jesus, His mother and brothers, and the disciples, left for Capernaum 'cuz no one had time for dallying.

It was after this that Jesus went preaching and teaching. Once, even, He had to throw a few brothers out of the church 'cuz they were using the church for selling sheep and cows and for lending money. Then He preached to the brothers there. When He was asked for proof, for a miracle, He said, *"Destroy this temple, and in three days I will raise it up."*

They didn't believe Him because it had taken forty-six years to build. But He wasn't talkin' 'bout a building, but His body, which rose from the dead after three days.

It's Gonna Take A Miracle

One Pharisee brother named Nicodemus came to Jesus one night. "Look, Teach," he said to Jesus, "You gotta be the Man 'cuz nobody could do these things unless he was on the one with the Almighty."

"For sure. Unless a brother is born again he can't even get in the Almighty's front door."

"What's with this born again? How can I go back inside my Momma? Are you saying this can be done?"

"Unless a brother is born of water and Spirit he can't get in the front door. Look, we ain't talking about flesh things, but spirit. Don't look so silly when I tell you 'you

gotta be born again.' You don't ask where the wind is coming from and you can hear it. Well, you don't have to know how, just know that being born again can be done."

"But, how?" Nicodemus asked. "It don't make sense."

"You're supposed to be the teacher. How can you not know?" Jesus answered him. "Look, you guys don't even seem to understand things when they are right in your face. How you gonna understand heavenly things? I came down from heaven to get things straight. Moses lifted up a serpent[91] and as the Son of Man, I gotta be lifted up too. It's this simple. The Almighty loved you guys so much that He sent His own kid so that you all could have that ever, always, and forever, kind of life. He didn't send the kid to give folks a hard time, but so that the kid could help save 'em. Some brothers will take the hard way 'cuz they're hardheaded. If they wanna stay in darkness rather than light, so be it. Evil don't like goodness and doesn't want to be around it. But if you're looking for the right road, you'll do the right thing and it'll be on the one with the Almighty."

And John the Baptist backed up Jesus all the way. When those wanna-be brothers wanted to know who this Jesus was, John said, "I ain't the Christ, but I came a little bit before Him. Now Jesus will be on the top and I'm being deep sixed, but it is as it should be 'cuz the Almighty don't make no mistakes."[92]

Afterwards it got back to Jesus that the Pharisees were hipped to the fact that Jesus was baptizing more folks

---

[91]See Numbers, Chapter 21, verse 9.
[92]See John, Chapter 3, verses 22 through 36.

than John the Baptist.[93] So, Jesus left Judea and headed
back to Galilee, one step ahead of the Pharisees always. He
crossed through the City of Samaria, which was the land
that Jacob had given to his boy, Joseph. In fact, the well
Jacob dug was still standing which is where Jesus ran into
a Samaritan sister getting water for her group.

"Sister, girl. Let me have some water, please." (Jesus
had sent His boys into town for food.)

And the sister wanted to know why Jesus was asking
her anything. "What gives with you, a Jew, asking me to
give You some water? Jews and Samaritans don't get
along."

*"If you knew 'bout the gift of the Almighty, you'd be
asking Me for a drink, and get hold of some living water."*

The sister looked around and said, "But You don't have
nothing to drink with. How can You give me living water?"

*"I ain't talking 'bout this water. Drink from here and
in a little while you'll want some more. But if you drink of
the water I'm talking 'bout you won't ever be thirsty again.
'Cuz this water gets you the all the way live. It the best in
living water."*

"I want some of that," the sister said.

"No problem. Go get your ol' man and come back."

"Got no one to call my ol' man," she answered.

*"That's cool, sister, 'cuz in truth you've had, count 'em,
five ol' men and the brother you're with now ain't your
husband. I like that you've told the truth."*

"You've gotta be an all right prophet," she said. "Our
dads worshipped on this mountain and you Jews say that

---

[93]Really it was the disciples who were baptizing with water
at this time, but of course that didn't matter to the
Pharisees. They continued to blame Jesus for everything.

Jerusalem is where a person oughta worship the Almighty."

"Yeah, that's true. But, sister, the time is coming when you won't worship on this mountain or Jerusalem 'cuz you don't really know what you're doing. Yeah, the time is coming when the true folks will worship the Almighty in a new way, in truth and light. You gotta worship the Almighty in a truly righteous fashion, in the spirit and in the truth."

"Well, I do know that one day the true messenger of the Almighty is gonna come. When He gets here, He'll set things straight."

"I speaking to you now," He told the sister. Just as He was talking with the sister, His boys came back from town. They didn't ask any questions, though they thought it strange that Jesus was talking to a Samaritan.

The woman was so excited she left her water jug and ran into town giving the lowdown on Jesus. "Ya'll gotta come see. He knew everything about me. You think the brother is the Christ?"

And the folks followed her back to check Him out. In the meantime, Jesus sat 'round while the brothers tried to get Him to eat. He told them that there was no need to eat 'cuz His food came from the Almighty.[94]

That day many brothers and sisters of Samaria were convinced that Jesus had to be the One. It wasn't just 'cuz the sister believed, but because they heard Jesus with their own ears and He convinced them.

From there Jesus went back to Galilee and things went well there, too. He went to Cana and healed a rich

---

[94]See John, Chapter 4, verses 31 through 38.

brother's kid. The brother had begged Jesus to heal his son, but Jesus said, *"Ya'll don't believe nothing unless you see it."*

"Please, come and heal my son," he begged.

"Your kid is already up and running."

And 'cuz the brother believed Jesus, so it was done. When he got there the servants told him, "Don't know how or why, but the kid is well."

This was the second sign Jesus did in Judea.

Later he healed a brother who was paralyzed. Not one brother would help him into the pool even though everybody who went in had been healed or cured. Jesus just said the word to the brother and in a flash, he was up and running, too!

The Pharisees were still out to do Jesus in, though. No matter how much good He did. They used lame excuses like, "The brother works on Sunday. Ain't nobody suppose to work on Sunday." Even though Jesus was doing good, they still wanted to lay Jesus out.

Jesus had to get them straight about what He was doing, but the brothers were full of themselves and their hearts were heavy with their tremendous egos. Even though Jesus explained how things worked, those Pharisees still thought they were hot stuff and knew all the answers.[95]

"If you are listening and believe what you're hearing about Me and the Almighty, you ain't got nothing to worry 'bout. It ain't nothing but a God thing happening 'round here and if you're ready, it's gonna be cool. But if you

---

[95]See John, Chapter 5, verses 19 through 23. Also, see Matthew, Chapter 3, verse 17.

wanna go 'round dissing Me and the Almighty, remember payback's a monster.

"All a person gotta do is look and the real deal is clear as a bell. Eat of Me and you ain't ever gonna be hungry again."

But the brothers wanted to know what He was talking 'bout.

"How can somebody give us His body to eat. I know that ain't right."

And Jesus heard them talking among themselves, whispering in the dark. He knew they wouldn't understand that His flesh was food and His blood was drink.[96]

This turned some folks off. So, some of those that had promised to follow Him, turned their back 'cuz all of this was just too hard to understand. But Jesus was already hip to the fact they didn't understand.

Jesus told them all, *"This ain't just Me saying these things, but My Father in Heaven, the Almighty, Hisself! Moses told you folks what was happening, and now you wanna kill Me? It don't make sense, but it's gotta be that way. Don't judge by appearances. Look deep."*

But every once in a while, folks said just maybe the brother was the Christ 'cuz who else could do what He did. In the end, however, the Pharisees thought they had the last word 'cuz they said, "It ain't so." And because of that some folks didn't know that Jesus was the One.

---

[96]See John, Chapter 6, verses 53 through 58.

The Pitch

A sister was caught doing the wild thing with somebody who wasn't her ol' man and the people in town decided she had to pay.

"Jesus," they yelled. "Whata ya say? This sister was caught dead in the act. The law says we gotta stone her to death."

Jesus stopped and started writing in the sand. He knew they were testing Him 'cuz they always were. And the brothers had crowded 'round now 'cuz they wanted to see what was going down. They wanted blood.

"Anybody who ain't never done nothing wrong in his life, go ahead. Toss a stone at her."

Then He bent down and started writing in the dirt again.

One by one the crowd started disappearing 'cuz there wasn't one without sin in the group. Not one. It wasn't long before it was just Jesus and the sister.

"Hmmm. Where's everybody? Nobody here to execute you?"

"Uh, uh," the sister said quietly.

"You've got nothing to worry 'bout with Me, neither. Go on and don't be doing that thing no more. Okay?" Then He said, *"I'm the light of this world and anybody who follows Me, the light gonna shine on them too!"*

The Pharisees were outdone. Who was Jesus to be saying something like that. It was one thing to have others bragging on Him, but for Him to brag on Himself made them mad.

But Jesus told them, *"You don't know Me or My Father. What do you know?"*

Later, Jesus told the folks that He was gonna be wasted. And then He explained the real deal to them all over again. He let them know that not everything was to be understood 'cuz folks in the dark, living that kind of life, sometimes stayed where they were. They didn't want to come out of darkness and so they didn't.

Some folks believed Him and others didn't 'cuz they were hardheaded, but Jesus told the brothers, *"You listen to what I say, you're My posse, My disciples. And because you're Mine, you'll know the truth when you see it, and the truth will make you free indeed."*

A brother was brought to Jesus who was blind. And the folks wanted to know who had done wrong, the brother or his parents.

"Neither. The brother is blind 'cuz the Almighty gonna show you His stuff. Don't you know I gotta work while it's day 'cuz when it's dark, you can't work. As long as I'm here, it's daytime for everybody."

Then He made the brother whole, but the Pharisees didn't want any part of it. They considered themselves Moses' folks and they didn't know or want to know Jesus. They asked the fixed-up brother who Jesus was, trying to convince him that Jesus was a devil. But the brother wasn't buying into it, so the Pharisees dumped him from the church roll. And they threw the brother out.[97]

Again, this was another sign. The brother was once in darkness and because of Jesus, he could now see the light. No brother could turn him away. And He told the Pharisees, *"You're more blind than this brother ever was."*

---

[97]See John, Chapter 9, verses 13 through 34.

I'm Gonna Get 'Cha

Jesus told the brothers, *"I am The One. I'm the door to the good things. Enter here and you're gonna be saved. Anybody else is just a thief in the night trying to rob you guys of your soul.*

"This is the real deal. A thief ain't interested in nothing but what he can take from you and he'll waste you if he can 'fore he lets you alone. I'm My Father's Kid and I've come to do right by you. I'm the owner's son 'cuz if I were just a manager, I might let a thief have whatever is yours 'cuz what is it to Me? But that ain't the case at all. I'm the One and I've got your back all the time."

And folks were divided on how to feel. Some felt it was on the one what He said, and others felt the brother Jesus had to be loose in the head. Even though Jesus tried to explain it all, some listened and some didn't. In the end, the ones who didn't listen looked for ways to waste Jesus 'cuz everything He was saying made them look bad.[98]

The Story Of Lazarus

Jesus' friends, Mary and Martha, had a favorite brother named Lazarus. And Lazarus took sick and was dying. Mary and Martha pleaded with Jesus 'cuz they knew He loved Lazarus, too.

"Please, come see 'bout Lazarus, Jesus. We don't want him to die."

And Jesus told them not to worry. *"This sickness is not the dying kind. Don't worry. Whatever will happen will be to the glory of the Almighty."*

---

[98]See John, Chapter 10, verses 31 through 39.

Jesus hung 'round a couple more days before heading to Judea. His boys wanted to know what was wrong since Jesus knew they wanted to waste Him there. But Jesus warned them not to worry 'cuz He was the light. In the dark, those wanna-be brothers would fail unless He said differently. Then Jesus told them that He had to go and wake Lazarus up.

When Jesus got to Lazarus' house, the funeral had already taken place 'cuz Lazarus had died while Jesus was away. Jesus told them He was glad that He hadn't come early 'cuz now they could watch Him work.

Jesus had them take Him to Lazarus' grave even though Martha was upset that her brother had died.

"You know, Jesus, if you had been there, Lazarus would still be here," she said sadly.

But Jesus understood. *"Don't worry, sister. Your brother will rise."*

Martha said, "Yes, I know. Glory, 'cuz he'll rise in the resurrection in the last day."

But Jesus said, *"Nope, that's not what I mean, Martha. I'm the resurrection and the life. I got the power."* And then He set out to show just what He meant. Jesus had Mary and Martha take Him to where Lazarus was buried.

Then Jesus came to the tomb and told them to open it up.

Martha hesitated. "Jesus, I'm sure it stinks in there. Lazarus has been dead for a while."

But Jesus wouldn't hear of them not believing Him. He insisted that they move it immediately. And when they had, Jesus first thanked the Almighty and then He called out, *"Hey, Lazarus, my brother. Come on out of there."*

It was a sight. All bound up with tape and cloth, Lazarus came hopping out of the tomb and everybody was amazed.

"Let him out of those things," Jesus urged.   Many brothers who saw this now believed.

And just like His boys had warned, those Pharisees tried to have Jesus killed, but Jesus was too slick for them.

Later, Jesus sat with Lazarus. While they were there this sister Mary came and poured some expensive wine on Jesus' head to the dismay of the brothers.[99]

But Jesus shushed them 'cuz He knew the sister was doing right by Him since it was only a matter of time before He let the Pharisees catch up to Him and waste Him. Not only that, those Pharisees were even plotting to kill Lazarus. Because of what Jesus had done for him, lots of folks had started to believe.

The next day Jesus came into Jerusalem, and folks took branches of palm trees, lay 'em in the road, and went out to meet Him, yelling "Hosanna! Bless the brother who comes in the name of the Almighty.   He's the King of Israel."

And Jesus sat on a donkey and rode into town just like it said in the Good Book before.[100]

Jesus let his boys know that it was time. He didn't need to run anymore 'cuz now the Almighty was gonna put a cap on the plan. He was gonna be wasted. So, He told this to the brothers, but they didn't want believe it. They felt they still needed Him. They just didn't get it.

---

[99]See Mark, Chapter 14, verses 4 to 7.
[100]See Matthew, Chapter 21, verse 7. Also, see Zachariah, Chapter 9, verse 9.

Jesus laid out the word of the past so they could get on with the future. He knew what He was doing 'cuz He trusted in the Almighty.[101]

Later, Jesus and his boys had a special last supper.[102] At the supper, He poured water into a tub and started washing the brothers' feet. But Peter didn't want Him to because he felt it wasn't right. Jesus just laid it all for him 'cuz He knew he didn't understand. Then Jesus let them know one of them was gonna betray him, but not everybody else knew who. Only Jesus and Judas were hipped to the fact that Judas was gonna help deliver Jesus to his enemies.[103] And after He let Judas know He knew, Judas left into the dark to do the deed.

Jesus told the brothers that there was one more commandment He wanted to add and that was, *"Ya'll gotta love one another as much as I have loved you. You'll know if you are My boys if you love each other."*

Then He told Peter he would deny Him. Peter, of course, said he'd never do that, but in the end, he found out Jesus was right.[104] Then Jesus told 'em everything else that was gonna happen over the next few days. Jesus told them that His dying was good 'cuz it would end up being the ultimate gift.[105]

"Don't sweat the small stuff, brother. If you believe in the Almighty, you gotta believe in Me. Don't you know that My Father's got a crib of cribs. There are so many you

---

[101] See Chapter 12, verses 39 through 50.
[102] See Matthew, Chapter 26, verse 2.
[103] See Luke, Chapter 22.
[104] See Mark, Chapter 14. Also, see John, Chapter 14.
[105] See John, Chapter 14, verses 25 through 31.

can't count. *If it wasn't on the one, I would have let you know. Just know that I'm going to make things righteous for you. You know where I'm going and how it's going down, too.*" He also let them know that He was the One. This was something they should have no doubt about. And He added that folks would hate them just like they hated Him 'cuz their eyes and ears were closed to the truth.[106]

Thomas wasn't so sure, though. "What cha talking 'bout? I don't get this. How can I know where You're going?"

Jesus answered him. *"I'm the way, the truth and the life. You can't touch the Almighty unless you come through Me. You know Me, you know My Father. What you see in Me is what you get with the Almighty."*

So Philip piped up, "All You gotta do is show us and it'll be on the one."

"Ain't I been here long enough for you to know Me, Philip? You been paying attention? You see Me, you see the Almighty. I'm in the Almighty and the Almighty is in Me 'cuz it wouldn't go down this way unless it was so.

"Look, you love Me, do the right thing. And if you're trying, I'm gonna lay a gift on you, a helper, that will keep you in the tough times. When I'm not here in the flesh, you'll still be one to one with Me. You love Me? Yeah, you do. Then you love the Almighty.

"I'm laying peace on you, brothers. Peace like you've never known. I gotta go home 'cuz the Almighty is tougher than I am, but I had to come. I just had to 'cuz the world needed to know about this. You get it?

---

[106]See John, Chapter 15 and 16. Also, see Matthew, Chapter 11 and Chapter 15.

"I'm the vine. The Almighty is the tailor of the vine. Anybody ain't doing the right thing is being taken from Me 'cuz we don't have time for the dumb stuff. Look brothers, you're My posse, the branches of this tree. So that The Almighty comes out looking good, you gotta go and do a good job 'cuz He's giving you everything He's got!

"I know how tough it's gonna be. You gotta be protected, but even though I'm not here I've got your back. In fact, it'll be better than when I was here. Brothers, I'm telling you that I had to come 'cuz otherwise those wanna-be, hardheaded folks who've been dissing Me and the Almighty for so long would have just kept on doing what they'd been doing. They would have been thinking that they were right to do it, too. But now that I've been here, they ain't got no excuse for doing the wrong thing. They can 'just say no' if they want to, but they don't and now they're gonna get paid. And," He told them, "they can't say they weren't warned.

"I know you don't want Me to go, but it's gotta be this way. The Almighty's working His plan big time. You will remember soon enough and understand better than before. I got a lot more to say, but you can't digest the full story so just be patient 'cuz in little while, it'll be clear."

Have A Little Talk

Later that evening, Jesus got one to one with the Almighty. He said, *"Dad, it's Me, Your son. I wanna thank you for letting Me come here. You were right as always. Now, I want You to help these brothers 'cuz you know things are gonna get rough. I ain't of this world, but these brothers are. It's one thing when I'm around to guide them, now they're gonna need You big time. I don't want You to take them out of the world, just don't let them mess up.*

"And, Daddy. I ain't just talking 'bout My boys 'cuz You know what's in My heart. No, sir. I'm talking 'bout everybody who believes in Me. I mean everybody that wants to share a piece of You, You gotta give it to 'em. I've told 'em all about You and that if they call on You, You'll be there."[107]

And afterward, they came to get Him just like He predicted. Right there on Gethsemane, Judas brought the soldiers to take Jesus away. Just as they started to handcuff Jesus, Peter took out his sword and cut off one of the brothers' right ear. The brother's name was Malchus. But Jesus wasn't having it, and made Peter drop his sword.

"Hey, brother. I gotta swallow this pill. It's gonna make things better."

Jesus went before the preachers and their crew on trumped-up charges, so He said nothing to them. At the same time, Peter sat there denying he even knew Jesus just like Jesus had said.

Next, they sent Jesus to the courthouse for a fake trial, and the folks found Him guilty (although He wasn't guilty of anything). But Jesus was cool. He went through all these hard times 'cuz He had the best interest of the world on His mind.[108]

"I ain't never hid from you guys. You got the lowdown on everything I've ever said or did, so why do you ask Me these lame questions? You wanna know what I'm all

---

[107] See John, Chapter 17.
[108] See, Mark, Chapter 14. Also, see Matthew, Chapter 26.

*about? Ask the folks. If you think I'm evil, then I should
be punished. If not, what's up with you sweating Me this
way?"*

And it was a hard time for Jesus. Not only were the
charges trumped up and the trial a sham, Jesus was spit on
and beat up 'cuz they wanted to humiliate the brother for
everybody to see. They called themselves proving that
Jesus wasn't who He said He was. But they were only
working the Almighty's plan. He told them, *"You think
you're doing this, but you couldn't touch Me if the
Almighty hadn't worked it out this way."*

Even after they took Him and put Him on the cross,
Jesus didn't try and save Himself 'cuz He was doing this
for the world. The soldiers put a sign above his head that
said, JESUS OF NAZARETH, KING OF THE JEWS. The
preachers didn't like that. They went immediately to
Pilate to get it changed.

"Don't say, 'King of the Jews,' tell them that He said He
was king."

But Pilate had it his way. "I want it up there. Leave it
alone."

Jesus' mother, his friends, Mary and Mary Magdalene
and the disciples whom He loved, stood before Him before
He died. He turned to His disciples and told them that now
they were all family. *"Mom, this is your son,"* He said to
His mother. To one disciple He said, *"This is now your
Mom, man."* Then He said, *"I thirst."* This was so that the
Scriptures could be fulfilled. They gave Him sour wine.
Then He died.

They buried Jesus in a tomb, but on the third day He
rose just like He said. And He went to the disciples and let
them see Him before He headed back to the Almighty.

Now one of the twelve was named Thomas and Thomas didn't believe that Jesus had risen from the dead. He wouldn't believe until he could see the wounds in Jesus' hands and feet. Well, several days later, Jesus showed up at one of their gatherings and sure enough, He went straight to Thomas.

"Okay, my brother Thomas. Touch so you can believe. I'm doing this so you can believe, but I'm telling you, man, the brother or sister who believes without seeing is gonna be blessed beyond belief."[109]

The Final Message

Jesus hung around for a bit, but several days later the boys (minus Judas 'cuz he had hung himself) were out near the sea when Jesus strolled up to them. He asked them if they had any food, and they said no. So He told them to throw out their net.

Now Peter knew who He was and he did as he was told and when they brought in the net it was full of fish. Jesus showed them that even though it was busting out all over with fish, the net could hold.

Later, Jesus asked Peter if he loved Him.

"You know I do, Jesus man. I do."

"Then feed my young folks, the lambs."

Then Jesus asked him a second and third time and each time Peter said, "Yes," Jesus said, *"Then feed and tend to my folks."* Peter was given a chance to make things right again.

---

[109] See John, Chapter 12, verses 24 through 29.

There was much that Jesus did and all the brothers talked about it. Some even wrote about it, but the whole world couldn't hold all the things that Jesus did even if everything was written down.

The end of the Book of John.
May the Almighty bless the reading of His Word!

About the Interpreter

P. K. McCary is an author, journalist, lecturer and stage artist.   Her books include the *Black Bible Chronicles: From Genesis to the Promised Land.*

As a journalist, Ms. McCary has reported for major newspapers and television stations across the country, in Houston, Denver, Washington, DC, and Atlanta.

She was deeply influenced by the spiritual teachings of her grandfather, a minister in Spencer, Oklahoma, whom she credits for instilling in her an abiding faith that "life is a spiritual connection with God."

Ms. McCary is the mother of three children and resides with them in Houston, Texas.